Sir James Melville: Scottish Ambassador

A Tudor Times Insight

By Tudor Times

Published by Tudor Times Ltd

## Tudor Times Insights

Tudor Times Insights are books collating articles from our website www.tudortimes.co.uk which is a repository for a wide variety of information about the Tudor and Stewart period 1485 – 1625. There you can find material on People, Places, Daily Life, Military & Warfare, Politics & Economics and Religion. The site has a Book Review section, with author interviews and a book club. It also features comprehensive family trees, and a 'What's On' event list with information about forthcoming activities relevant to the Tudors and Stewarts.

**Titles in the Series**

*Profiles*

*People*

*Politics & Economy*

# Contents

## Sir James Melville: Scottish Ambassador

## Introduction

James Melville was one of many ambassadors employed by the Scottish Crown to manage relations with England. He knew everyone with influence at both courts. James began his career in the household of Mary, Queen of Scots in France. After a brief military excursion, he became a diplomat and travelled widely until returning to Scotland in 1564.

While there is little known about Melville's private life, he was at the heart of a network of family and co-religionists who were at the centre of affairs in both England and Scotland. Like others of his generation, he believed in witchcraft, and became embroiled in one of the more bizarre incidents of James VI's reign.

In his domestic life, Melville did not move far from his birthplace in Fife, but in his public career he travelled extensively on the continent, as well as frequently journeying between Edinburgh and London.

Part 12 contains Sir James Melville's Life Story and additional information about him, looking at different aspects of his life. On excellent terms with most of the leading figures of the day, he left a fascinating memoir of his life – although, reading between the lines, he wasn't always as straightforward as he seems. Was he a diplomat, or a spy?

# Family Tree

## Sir James MELVILLE of Halhill

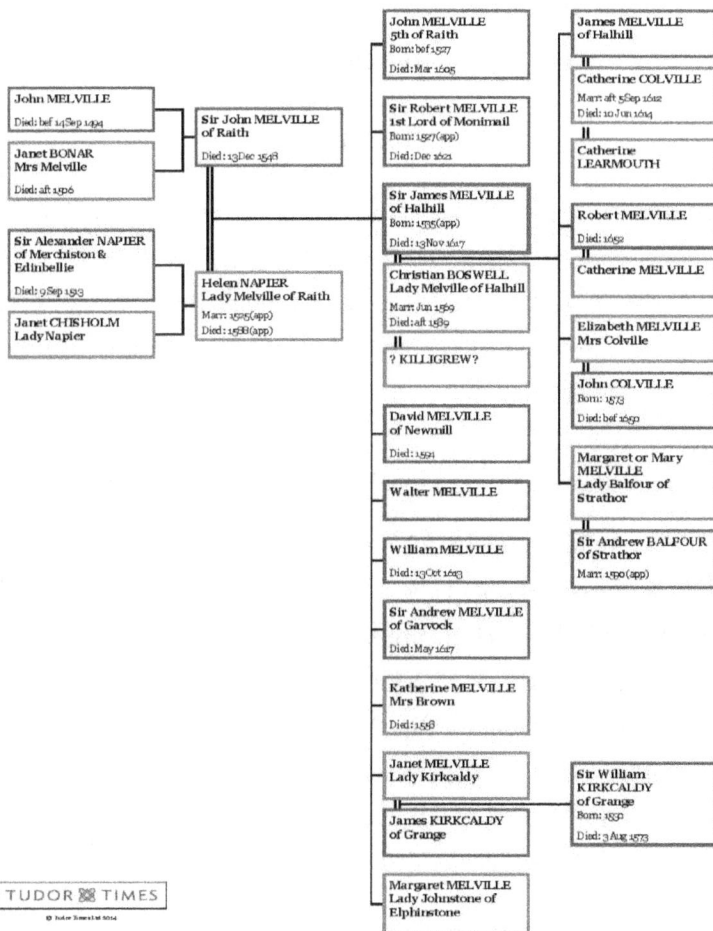

**John MELVILLE**
Died: bef 14 Sep 1494

**Janet BONAR**
Mrs Melville
Died: aft 1506

**Sir Alexander NAPIER**
of Merchiston &
Edinbellie
Died: 9 Sep 1513

**Janet CHISHOLM**
Lady Napier

**Sir John MELVILLE**
of Raith
Died: 13 Dec 1548

**Helen NAPIER**
Lady Melville of Raith
Marr: 1525 (app)
Died: 1558 (app)

**John MELVILLE**
5th of Raith
Born: bef 1527
Died: Mar 1605

**Sir Robert MELVILLE**
1st Lord of Monimail
Born: 1527 (app)
Died: Dec 1621

**Sir James MELVILLE**
of Halhill
Born: 1535 (app)
Died: 13 Nov 1617

**Christian BOSWELL**
Lady Melville of Halhill
Marr: Jun 1589
Died: aft 1589

**? KILLIGREW ?**

**David MELVILLE**
of Newmill
Died: 1591

**Walter MELVILLE**

**William MELVILLE**
Died: 13 Oct 1643

**Sir Andrew MELVILLE**
of Garvock
Died: May 1617

**Katherine MELVILLE**
Mrs Brown
Died: 1598

**Janet MELVILLE**
Lady Kirkcaldy

**James KIRKCALDY**
of Grange

**Margaret MELVILLE**
Lady Johnstone of
Elphinstone

**James MELVILLE**
of Halhill

**Catherine COLVILLE**
Marr: aft 5 Sep 1612
Died: 10 Jun 1614

**Catherine**
LEARMOUTH

**Robert MELVILLE**
Died: 1652

**Catherine MELVILLE**

**Elizabeth MELVILLE**
Mrs Colville

**John COLVILLE**
Born: 1573
Died: bef 1652

**Margaret or Mary**
MELVILLE
Lady Balfour of
Strathor

**Sir Andrew BALFOUR**
of Strathor
Marr: 1590 (app)

**Sir William**
KIRKCALDY
of Grange
Born: 1532
Died: 3 Aug 1573

## Sir James Melville's Life Story

## Chapter 1: Memoirs

The memoirs left by Sir James Melville, written after he had retired from public life in 1603 make fascinating reading. Melville clearly has a sense of humour, and a readable style, although the sixteenth century Scots in which he wrote takes some getting used to. Scots is a Germanic dialect, similar to English but with different spelling, pronunciation and vocabulary. It was (and is) spoken in Lowland Scotland. Highland Scotland was still largely Gaelic speaking in the sixteenth century.

Melville wrote his memoirs for his children, and there are quite a few discursions addressed to them about how princes should govern and how honest men should live. These are interesting as reflecting the morality of the time, particularly as Melville was a Protestant in an era when religious life changed dramatically. His early childhood in the 1530s was in a nation still Catholic, although his native Fife was one of the first parts of the country to embrace the reformed faith, and his father was an early adherent of George Wishart, the most notable reformer in Scotland prior to John Knox.

By the 1580s the Presbyterian Kirk ruled every aspect of people's lives. Melville himself, although Protestant, seems to have been unusually tolerant in the matter of other people's religion, and, although he comments occasionally that someone is a '*Papist*' he does not seem to hold it against anyone. Like most of his contemporaries, most notably his king, James VI, he believed in witches and witchcraft.

Much of what we know of relations between Mary, Queen of Scots and her cousin, Elizabeth of England, has been derived from Melville's anecdotes, and his proximity to both people and events give a rich store of information about the complex political manoeuvrings of the time.

On the surface, Melville's memoirs appear to be frank and straightforward. He was a warm supporter of Mary, Queen of Scots, until, at her deposition, he accepted reality and transferred his allegiance to her baby son, always with the caveat that, should Mary be freed from her captivity in England, he would wish her to be returned to her throne. However, continued reading, and comparison of names and events with surviving correspondence from Melville and others suggest that he may not, in fact, have been quite such a devoted follower of the Queen's as he claimed.

Whilst it is not possible to deduce anything with certainty (so far as our current research has gone) the possibility that he was working with Mary's half-brother, the Earl of Moray, and Sir William Cecil in England, to destabilise Mary's government cannot be ignored.

The following life story therefore, whilst based on his memoirs, identifies some incidents where he may not have been entirely honest (although, it is possible, of course, that forty years after the events he was describing, he may have genuinely forgotten or misremembered facts).

Disappointingly, Melville gives absolutely no information about his personal life, other than references to his brothers.

## Chapter 2: Youth

The Melville family was settled in Fife, a reasonably prosperous part of the Kingdom of Scotland, to the north-east of Edinburgh.

Melville's father, Sir John Melville of Raith, Captain of Dunbar Castle, was an early Scottish convert to Protestantism and supported the pro-English party in Scotland that sought to unite Britain through a marriage between the Queen, Mary, and Prince Edward of England. One of the obstacles to this plan was Cardinal Beaton. Beaton was assassinated, with covert encouragement from the English, in 1546, but, although Sir John was associated with some of the assassins, he was not directly involved, and after the disastrous battle of Pinkie Cleugh in 1547, was dispatched to England to make terms. Whilst there, he shared information with the English government about Scottish and French military dispositions. For this treason, he was executed and his lands forfeited in December 1548.

One of the other men associated with the assassination of Beaton, and the pro-English faction, because of his strong religious affiliation with the Reformers, was Henry Balnaves of Halhill, near Kirkcaldy in Fife. Kircaldy was close to Raith, and according to John Knox, Sir John Melville was an early patron of Balnaves. This support was returned when Balnaves at some unknown time, but before 1569, adopted James Melville.

It is unknown what Melville's early education consisted of, but we can probably assume he learnt to read and write in Scots, Latin and French, and that he was brought up in the Reformed Faith, as it was being preached by the Scots Reformer George Wishart, and later, John Knox.

Despite the association of the Melvilles with the pro-English party, in late 1549, when Jehan de Monluc, Bishop of Vallance who had been sent to Scotland as Ambassador from the French King was returning home, thirteen year old James Melville was chosen to accompany him. He was to join the household of the young Mary, Queen of Scots who had been sent to France for safe-keeping, and with the intention of marrying her to the Dauphin François.

The journey to France was made via the west coast, with the objective of Vallance meeting the Irish lords who were trying to throw off English overlordship, preferring to be subject to Catholic France. The voyage was beset by storms, and the ship was obliged to shelter from the storm on a small island for thirteen days. By *'Fastrons Eve'* – that is, Shrove Tuesday, they reached Loch Foyle and were welcomed by the clan chief O'Dochartaigh.

The trip to Ireland obviously amused Melville. He recorded that the Bishop had been making eyes at O'Dochartaigh's daughter, so a *'harlot'* was brought to him secretly. Whilst she was waiting for him in his room, she found a small box of liquid, sitting on the window ledge, drying out after being soaked during the storm. She consumed it, licking the entire contents out of the box. Vallance, when he came in, let out a cry of annoyance, and so his plan to break his vows of celibacy was discovered. He was angry because the liquid was some rare and precious balm of Egypt, that had been given to him as a gift by the Sultan of Turkey, following an embassy there.

Meanwhile, the daughter of O'Dochartaigh who had been running away from Vallance, was running after Melville. She offered to marry him and go away with him anywhere he chose. He fended her off, thanking her for her kind offer, but telling her he was too young, and had no income, and, in any event was en route to France in his Queen's service.

After about three weeks of negotiations in Ireland, the party returned to Dumbarton. Following a short digression to Stirling to take leave again of the Dowager Queen, Marie of Guise, the party sailed from Dumbarton for France, via the Isle of Man, in two French ships. These vessels were returning to France after delivering money to pay the soldiers defending Scotland against the English in the War of the Rough Wooing.

After eight days at sea, Melville and the rest arrived at Le Conquet, in Brittany. Vallance hurried ahead to Paris, leaving Melville to travel in more comfort, furnishing him with enough money to buy horses and pay expenses for himself and two Scottish gentleman, his companions.

The trio fell in with two Frenchman and a Spaniard and decided to travel together in a journey that is reminiscent of every young traveller's experience over the centuries. On the first night, the six shared a room in an inn, two to a bed. Melville sharing with the Spaniard. In the middle of the night he heard the two Scotsmen plotting to tell Vallance that the journey had cost twice as much as it did, to cover their own expenses. Then he heard the Frenchmen planning to take advantage of the others not speaking French to bamboozle them over the prices. Narrowly missing being mugged by a couple of cronies of the two Frenchmen, Melville finally made it to Paris just after Easter 1550.

Melville expected Vallance to introduce him to the Queen of Scots immediately, but, after a month, he still had not been taken to her, although Vallance made arrangements for him to improve his French and learn to play the lute. The Bishop even talked of adopting Melville, but nothing came of the idea.

Before being introduced to the Queen of Scots, Melville came to the attention of the Constable of France, the strangely named Anne de Montmorency, who, together with his ally Diane de Poitiers, strongly influenced Henri II. The Constable requested Melville to join his service, which Melville agreed to, provided the Bishop would let him go. Bishop Vallance agreed, and Melville became a servant of the Constable in May 1553.

## Chapter 3: Life in France

War was almost continuous between France and the Empire – sometimes in Italy, and sometimes in the area of Franco-Burgundian border. Melville accompanied the army led into Picardy by the Constable in 1553. The results of the various battles were inconclusive, and both armies fell back into winter quarters, with Melville returning to Chantilly with the Constable.

Attempts by Cardinal Reginald Pole (cousin to Mary I of England, soon to be Archbishop of Canterbury) to mediate between France and the Empire were unsuccessful. In 1554 Henri II again advanced, and Melville, although still in the Constable's retinue, was granted a pension by the King. After a season of war and sieges, both sides claimed victory. A five year truce was then signed, to facilitate the Emperor Charles' decision to retire – handing over his Spanish, Burgundian and New World lands to his son, Philip II, and persuading the Imperial Electors to select his brother, Ferdinand, as the new Emperor.

Before the five years of truce were completed, the Pope, Paul IV, tried to persuade Henri II to break it, to support his campaign against Spain in Naples. This idea was taken up by the Guise brothers – François, Duke of Guise and Cardinal Charles of Lorraine, the uncles of the Queen of Scots. The Constable opposed the breaking of the truce but his advice was overridden and France advanced into both Naples and Picardy. The Guise brothers were then horrified to discover that the Pope had made a separate truce.

An angry Philip II prepared for war, persuading his wife, Mary I of England, to support him. The Anglo-Spanish and French armies, the latter including Melville, met at St Quentin where the Anglo-Spanish, under the Duke of Savoy achieved a resounding victory. Melville was wounded by a severe blow to the head, but managed to escape the field. He mentions being helped by a man he names as Henry Killigrew, describing him as an old friend. Killigrew, a Protestant, had been in exile in France since 1556. It is not clear which side Killigrew was fighting on, but, presumably, the French side.

Failing to follow up their victory, the tables were turned on the Anglo-Spanish when Henri II made a lightening swoop on Calais, capturing the town from the English garrison. Despite this victory, France was at a disadvantage, and was forced to make peace in the Treaty of Cateau-Cambresis.

Melville was present at proceedings, still serving the Constable, who had been captured at St Quentin. The French were divided amongst themselves – the Constable in favour of peace, which would release him from bondage, and the Guise party reluctant to have him back at court where they were increasing their influence. On this occasion, the Constable had the upper hand, but, at the urging of the Guise faction, the treaty encompassed oaths for France and Spain to try to restore the Catholic faith in parts of Europe where the Reformation had taken hold.

The English hoped to retain Calais, but, with Queen Mary now dead, Philip had less interest in England, and did not make restoration of the town a condition of peace. England received a sop in that Calais was to be restored after eight years, or a sum of 450,000 crowns paid for, it although it was apparent to all present that this would never happen. Scotland, whose Queen was married to the heir to the French throne, was encompassed in the peace.

With Queen Mary of England dead, there were many who thought that Mary, Queen of Scots was her legal heir, rather than Elizabeth, who had already been proclaimed queen and crowned. New silverware was ordered for the young Queen of Scots and her husband, the Dauphin, which was engraved with the arms of England. According to Melville, this was the idea of the Queen's uncle, the Cardinal of Lorraine. It proved to be one of the greatest mistakes the Queen (only sixteen at the time) ever made. The English were angry and protested but were put off with lame excuses.

The Scottish oath to observe the Treaty was to be sworn by the Regent, Marie of Guise. Originally, it was planned that Melville should return home to administer the oath, but it was decided to send a more influential figure who could persuade Queen Marie to step up persecution against Protestants – an action she had been unwilling to take. This undermining of Marie's policy of tolerance in return for support for her rule and for her absent daughter led to dissension, and revolt in Scotland, under the leadership of the Lords of the Congregation. The Lords, led by Mary's illegitimate half-brother, Lord James Stewart, had converted to Protestantism.

Henri II and the Constable agreed that Melville should return to Scotland to report on affairs. Melville was strictly charged by the Constable to determine whether it would be necessary for Henri II to send troops to support Queen Marie. Melville was to investigate whether the rebellion of the Lords of the Congregation was an attempt to overthrow the Queen and replace her with Lord James Stewart, or to protect the Protestant religion. If the latter, the Constable believed that France should not interfere.

So Melville returned to Scotland, via England. Once in Scotland, Melville hurried to Falkland Palace, to see Queen Marie. He was the introduced by Henry Balnaves (who had had his lands restored in 1556) to Lord James Stewart. The twenty-four year old Melville appears to have struck up a good relationship with Lord James, some four years his senior. Lord James assured Melville that he had no designs on the crown, and would be willing to live abroad to show that he was quite innocent of any improper ambitions. Melville, convinced by his sincerity, set out once again for France.

On his return to France, Melville passed through Newcastle in England, and recounts a strange tale that he picked up there. He met a man who claimed that Henry VIII, on being told that his son would die without children, tried to poison both his daughters, with the effect that, although neither died, they would both be barren. The tale seems quite extraordinary, but Melville appears to have believed it, and interprets other events on the assumption that it was true.

## Chapter 4: Travelling in Europe

On arrival in France, Melville found the political situation quite altered. Henri II was dead, and his son, the fifteen year old François, was now King, with Mary, Queen of Scots as his consort. The young couple were dominated by her Guise uncles, who were determined both to pursue their Catholic mission and to push forward their niece as the rightful Queen of England. Melville's master, the Constable, with his more conciliatory approach, had been banished from court.

With Mary of Scotland now being proclaimed as Queen of England, and the mustering of French troops to support Marie of Guise in Scotland, the Lords of the Congregation sought help from Elizabeth of England. Elizabeth was never inclined to help rebels, even if they were apparently her co-religionists, but she could not afford to tolerate Mary's impertinent use of her titles. The situation in Scotland deteriorated, and was close to open war when Queen Marie died. The Lords of the Congregation having gained the upper hand, the Scots in France came under suspicion. Melville decided to leave France and travel around Europe.

His first port of call was the court of the Elector Palatine. The Elector, Frederick III, was a staunch Calvinist and Melville found favour with him. It was not long, however, before Melville was back in France.

François II had died of an ear infection, leaving the Queen of Scots widowed at seventeen. The Guises were immediately dismissed from favour as the new king, Charles IX's, mother, Catherine de Medici became Regent of France. Constable Montmorency was back in favour.

Queen Mary, unloved by her mother-in-law, retired from court, and Melville returned to the Palatinate with messages from Queen Catherine to the Elector. Catherine was toying with the idea of joining a league with the Protestant princes of Europe, including Elizabeth of England, and the Elector, to counterbalance the faction of the Guises, and their ally, Philip of Spain.

With no place for her in France, Mary decided to return to Scotland where she took up personal rule, supported by her half-brother, Lord James, to whom she granted the Earldom of Moray, and Sir William Maitland of Lethington, who was a friend of Sir William Cecil, Secretary of State to Queen Elizabeth. The queens professed friendship and alliance and all seemed set fair.

Melville had journeyed from the Palatinate to France to swear allegiance to Mary before her departure. She told him he would be welcome in her service, should he wish to leave the Elector, but he returned to the Palatinate for the time being and continued to carry out diplomatic missions on the Elector's behalf.

The Elector was negotiating to marry his son, Prince Casimir, either to the sister of the Duke of Lorraine, or, failing that, to Queen Elizabeth. Melville recounted that he refused to negotiate a match with Elizabeth, as he knew she intended to remain single because of the poison he believed she had been given on her father's orders.

Melville then received orders to travel to the court of the Emperor Ferdinand to enquire into a marriage between Queen Mary and the Archduke Charles, Ferdinand's younger son. Ferdinand left much of the management of his affairs to his older son, Maximilian, King of the

Romans.  Maximilian was rumoured to be a Protestant, and was courting both the three Catholic Imperial Electors and the three Protestant ones (including the Elector Palatine) all of whom thought he was on their side of the religious fence.  It was thus believed by the Scottish court that Melville, as a servant of the Protestant Elector Palatine, would be warmly received by Maximilian.

Maximilian talked to Melville pressing him for every particular about the state of affairs in Scotland and whether the Scots would really wish to press Queen Mary's claim to England.  He remained with the King of the Romans for fifteen days.

Melville was not initially clear in his own mind what Maximilian thought about a marriage between his brother, Archduke Charles, and Queen Mary, but eventually concluded that Maximilian would prefer Charles to remain single, as, if he became King of Scots, and perhaps England, in right of his wife, Charles might be in a position to take Burgundy should Philip of Spain have no heirs, whilst currently, Maximilian, as the husband of Philip's sister, was likely to inherit.

On seeing that his embassy was likely to prove fruitless, Melville left Maximilian, and travelled to Venice and Rome before returning to the Elector's court at Heidelburg.

### Chapter 5: Back to France

Melville's next embassy was back to France.  Catherine de Medici was considering the Elector's daughter as a wife for Charles IX and Melville was despatched to deliver her picture and describe her charms to the French court.  He arrived at a court riven with faction.  The Constable was back in his old place, but he and Catherine de Medici were not on good terms, and nor was she on particularly good terms with Admiral

Coligny, leader of the Huguenot faction and the Constable's brother-in-law.

Melville was reprimanded for revealing his commission from the Elector to the Constable before informing Catherine and King Charles of the details, but was forgiven, and offered a place in the King's Privy Chamber. Whilst he was contemplating accepting the job, news came of a plot on Coligny's life – discovered by the Huguenot Duchess Renee of Ferrara (daughter of Louis XII of France and thus great-aunt to Charles IX, as well as mother to the now-widowed Duchess of Guise). The would-be assassin was himself found dead, and suspicion fell on the Constable and Coligny. At this point, Melville was relieved to receive a summons to return to Scotland to undertake commissions for Queen Mary.

He returned to the Elector before setting out for Scotland in 1564, and agreed to carry pictures of the young Prince Casimir to England. Casimir was still hoping Elizabeth would marry him, and Melville was still certain that she would not. Nevertheless, he was prepared to visit Elizabeth on Casimir's behalf, provided he was furnished with pictures of the whole family, not just Casimir, so that he could introduce the matter in a roundabout way.

As well as offering a husband she didn't want, Melville was also obliged to tell Elizabeth that the Protestant Electors, having agreed with Maximilian that he would declare himself a Protestant on the death of Ferdinand, had promised not to ally with any other monarchs. Should Maximilian go back on his word, they would be delighted to ally with Queen Elizabeth.

Elizabeth promised Melville that she wouldn't breathe a word of this to her Council, and they discussed the virtues of the Elector – this gave Melville the opportunity to show Elizabeth the picture of Casimir. She kept it overnight, but said that Lord Robert Dudley (the man half Europe believed she planned to marry) should be the judge of Casimir's suitability. Melville was confirmed in his opinion that Elizabeth would not marry Casimir, which he repeated by letter to the Elector.

Whilst he was at the English Court, Elizabeth talked much of her friendship for Queen Mary, and her desire to be treated as an older sister by the younger queen, saying that she would write on the topic to Melville with her own hand when he had returned to Scotland. In the meantime, Mary had written to Elizabeth, asking her opinion on a match between Mary and Archduke Charles.

Elizabeth, rather than writing to Melville, sent her thoughts on Mary's marriage by her own ambassador, Sir Thomas Randolph. She was quite clear that she would feel that the amity between the two queens would be undermined if Mary married Charles. Instead, she suggested that Mary should marry one of Elizabeth's own nobles. To make certain that the match with Charles would not take place, Elizabeth dispatched the Earl of Sussex to the Emperor's court (Maximilian was now Emperor) to hint that she herself might still be available – a far superior choice, as England was a good deal more prosperous than Scotland.

Elizabeth then made a proposition of another possible husband for Queen Mary who would please Elizabeth, and encourage her to nominate Mary as her successor. Her candidate was none other than Lord Robert Dudley, the mysterious death of whose first wife, Amy Robsart, had led Queen Mary to comment a couple of years before that

'The Queen of England [was] going to marry her horsemaster, who [had] murdered his wife to make room for her.'

Mary was angry and insulted – first, that Elizabeth was undermining her possible marriage to the Archduke, and, second, that she should think her own cast-off suitable for Mary.

Further distrust entered into the relationship when Matthew Stuart, Earl of Lennox, a Scot who had been exiled for many years in England was given leave to return home, much to the disquiet of the Lennox' hereditary enemies, the Hamiltons. Elizabeth advised Mary to beware of situations where rivalry between the factions could arise, but Mary, convinced that everything Elizabeth said had some ulterior, and damaging, motive, was chary of trusting her and wrote a letter that Elizabeth claimed to find offensive. It is easy to imagine the occasionally impetuous Mary dashing off a letter in the heat of her annoyance, and it appearing rude and ungrateful to Elizabeth, who rather fancied herself in the role of mentor to the younger woman.

Up until this point, Mary and Elizabeth had been corresponding in their own hands, with some regularity, but this now ceased, and there were no messages for a couple of months, until Mary decided to send Melville back to England to try to patch matters up, at least to outward appearance.

## Chapter 6: Embassy to England

Melville had intended to return either to the Palatinate or to France, to pursue his career there, as he was unimpressed by the factious state of Scotland. However, he was so charmed by Queen Mary, and so impressed with her 'princely virtues' that he felt it his duty to remain in her service, believing her to be 'more worthy to be served for little profit than any other prince in Europe for great commodity'. He thus accepted her commission, including a pension of 1,000 marks.

In late September of 1564 Mary sent Melville to England to treat with Elizabeth, to send messages to Lady Margaret Douglas (wife of the aforementioned Earl of Lennox) who was her father's half-sister, and to meet the Spanish Ambassador and Mary's other supporters.

The main purport of Mary's letters to Elizabeth was to try to smooth over the dispute that seemed to have arisen between them over the matter of Lennox. Melville was to tell Elizabeth that Mary had been grateful for her advice, and that if she had written anything that could be misinterpreted, he was to assure Elizabeth that only the most positive messages should be taken from Mary's letters. Mary could not actually remember what she had written – she didn't think it necessary to copy any *'familiar letters'* she wrote with her own hand.

The next matter was to agree a meeting between trusted councillors of both queens who would be able to resolve any disputes there might be.

Melville was then to tread carefully, and try to find out what was to be discussed in the forthcoming English Parliament. Mary was aware that Parliament was pressing Elizabeth to name a successor. Elizabeth had refused to do so, but perhaps Parliament would force her hand. In so far as Elizabeth was willing to opine on the succession, she had observed that she knew of no-one with a better right than Mary, but that was not exactly a ringing endorsement. Melville was to hint to Elizabeth that a failure to confirm Mary as her successor might lead people to believe that her protestations of friendship were mere words.

Melville arrived in London and took lodgings at Westminster. As soon as she heard of his arrival Elizabeth sent a message to say she would see him the next morning at 8 o'clock as she was walking in her garden. That evening, Sir Nicholas Throckmorton paid a visit. The Throckmortons were a large clan, based at Coughton Court in Warwickshire, and pretty equally divided between committed Catholics and steadfast Protestants.

Sir Nicholas was in the latter camp. Melville had first become acquainted with him when Throckmorton was Elizabeth's Ambassador to France during the reigns of Henri II and François II. The two were good friends, and Throckmorton had even chiselled a pension out of the notoriously parsimonious Elizabeth for Melville, during his time in Germany. It may seem quite extraordinary to us that Melville could receive a pension from Elizabeth whilst working for Mary, but no-one thought it at all strange at the time.

Throckmorton, although a Protestant, and highly favoured by Elizabeth, was one of her courtiers who supported Mary as her successor. Throckmorton's advice was that, should Elizabeth prove recalcitrant in the matter of naming Mary her heir, the sight of Melville cosying up to the Spanish Ambassador would concentrate her mind.

The next morning, Elizabeth sent a servant, a horse harnessed with velvet and two gentlemen, including Sir Thomas Randolph, who had been her Ambassador to Mary the previous year, to fetch Melville from his lodgings.

He met the Queen pacing up and down, as was her custom, in one of the alleys in the Palace gardens. They conversed in French, Melville being more comfortable in that than in his native Scots after so long away, and the Queen, although she might have understood Scots which was similar to English, was fluent in French. The first matter was Queen Mary's allegedly offensive letter.

Elizabeth brandished a response she had drafted – equally blunt and 'despiteful'. Melville, saying that Queen Mary could not remember what she had written, asked to see the original letter. Elizabeth let him read it. It was written in French, and Melville told Elizabeth that, although she spoke beautiful French, she could not be familiar with the everyday French that Mary wrote and spoke, which was rather less flowery between friends (such as he supposed the two queens to be) than Elizabeth might be used to.

Elizabeth allowed herself to be mollified, especially as Mary had made the first move in patching things up by sending Melville. She destroyed her draft letter, and promised to continue in loving friendship with Mary, interpreting anything the latter might do in the best possible light.

Elizabeth then moved on to talk of Mary's marriage. Had she come to any conclusion following Elizabeth's suggestion that she marry an English noble?

Melville answered that Mary had not given the matter any thought – waiting for a conference to be arranged to discuss the matter with all of the other business between the two countries. Mary would send Moray and Lethington, and hoped that Elizabeth would send the Earl of Bedford and Lord Robert Dudley.

Elizabeth pounced on Dudley's name, saying that Melville obviously held him of small account, as he had mentioned him second – but Elizabeth was going to ennoble him, in front of Melville's very eyes. Lord Robert, she added, was as dear as a brother and her best friend. She would have married him herself, if she felt inclined to marriage, but as it was, she thought him the best possible husband for Mary. If Mary did marry Dudley, Elizabeth would be very likely to name her as successor as she would then be free of all thought of being hurried to her end.

### Chapter 7: Fencing with Elizabeth I

Elizabeth was as good as her word in regard to Dudley, and Melville and the French Ambassador were invited to stand next to the queen and watch the ceremony in which he was promoted to Earl of Leicester and Baron Denbigh. Melville observed that, wrapping the peer's robe around him, Elizabeth could not resist tickling Dudley's neck. Not necessarily the way to promote his suitability as the husband of another woman.

After the ceremony, Elizabeth asked what Melville thought of Dudley, or Leicester, as he now was. Melville answered that the new earl was lucky to have a mistress who appreciated his talents. Elizabeth then went for the jugular.

'*Yet*,' she said, '*you like better of yonder long lad*,' pointing at Henry, Lord Darnley. Darnley was the son of the Earl of Lennox and his countess, Lady Margaret Douglas. Leaving aside Henry VIII's machinations with the succession in his will, Darnley was Elizabeth's nearest male heir and second after Queen Mary in a traditional pattern of inheritance.

Melville brushed off the accusation, saying that Darnley was a mere boy, even though he had a commission burning a hole in his pocket to treat with the Countess of Lennox about sending Darnley to Scotland to undertake some legal business with his father – and perhaps for Mary to look him over. The Countess had been intriguing for some time for Mary to marry her son.

Elizabeth was determined to pursue the idea of Mary marrying Leicester, so, as she said she could not talk to Mary directly, she would talk to Melville as familiarly. He remained at Westminster for nine days, and met the Queen at least once, and sometimes as frequently as three times, each day.

The two fenced verbally – Elizabeth pushing Leicester, and Melville indicating that Mary had not even heard the suggestion, and that it might all be discussed as part of a commission, when she had been named as Elizabeth's heir. Elizabeth countered with the impossibility of naming Mary unless she had shown herself willing to take Elizabeth's advice. Elizabeth had, however, commissioned lawyers to identify her legal successor – she did hope they would tell her it was Mary!

Melville brandished the fact that before the birth of his younger children, Henry VIII had contemplated leaving his throne to his nephew, James V (Mary's father) in default of male heirs (actually, Henry had stoutly resisted any such idea).

Elizabeth then told him that, if Mary did not co-operate, she would have to marry and have children herself. Melville, in an astonishing piece of plain speaking to a queen replied:

*'Madam, you need not tell me that. I know your stately stomach (disposition). You think if you were married, you would be but Queen of England. Now you are King and Queen both. You may not suffer (will not tolerate) a commander.'*

Elizabeth then showed Melville her miniature of Queen Mary – *'accidentally'* letting him see she also had one of Leicester. Melville asked for the latter to show Mary, on the grounds that Elizabeth had the original, but Elizabeth refused. He then asked for a large ruby that Elizabeth had been flaunting, to be sent as a token. The Queen again denied the request but added that one day Mary would have everything, if she followed Elizabeth's advice. She would, however, send a diamond.

It now being late, Melville was sent away to have his supper with a request to return to the gardens in the morning. At supper, he sat with Lady Stafford, one of the Queen's ladies-in-waiting, and a close friend as well as a relative of Elizabeth. Dorothy Stafford, paternal grand-daughter of Edward, Duke of Buckingham and maternal grand-daughter of Margaret Plantagenet, Countess of Salisbury, had married her cousin, Sir William Stafford, the widower of Elizabeth's aunt, Mary Boleyn, and been exiled in Geneva with other Protestants during Mary's reign.

Melville had known Lady Stafford and her daughter, Elizabeth, at the court of France, as they passed through en route to Geneva, and had struck up a warm friendship with the daughter. Both ladies were a source of information as to happenings at the English court.

Mary had instructed Melville to entertain Queen Elizabeth, so he told her stories of the countries he had visited, and about the clothes that the women wore – Elizabeth was well aware of the power of clothes to demonstrate power, and political allegiance, and wore clothes in French,

Italian and English styles.  Melville was asked which he liked best and responded that the Italian style was the most attractive – this was a play on the Queen's vanity, as Italian ladies showed their hair, and Elizabeth was proud of her curly red-gold locks.

Having begun a quasi-flirtation, Elizabeth then wanted to know who was the prettier, herself or Mary.  The silver-tongued Melville replied that the one was the prettiest queen in England, the other, the prettiest queen in Scotland.  Elizabeth pursued the matter and he told her she was the fairer-skinned, but Mary was '*lusome*' (attractive or desirable).  He was now backed into a corner with Elizabeth wanting to know who was the taller, what Mary did for exercise, and how well she played the virginals.  Mary's virtuosity, was '*reasonable, for a Queen,*' he replied.

Later that day, after his audience with the Queen was over, Melville was invited by her cousin, Lord Hunsdon, to take a walk in a gallery, into which the sounds of expertly played virginals were wafting.  He drew back a curtain to see the Queen, who, with her back to him, continued playing until she could no longer keep up the pretence of being unaware of his presence.  She took her hands from the keys and protested that she never played in front of gentlemen.

He excused his bad manners in intruding on her, and asked for punishment.  Elizabeth sat, and placing a cushion for him on the floor, and summoning Lady Stafford as chaperone, proceeded to quiz him on the relative charms of herself and Mary.  He had to admit that Elizabeth was the better musician.  Elizabeth then showed off her Italian (good, in his opinion) and German (not so good.)

## Chapter 8: Return to Scotland

By now, Melville was keen to return to Scotland.  Elizabeth complained that he had tired of her company, sooner than she had of his.

Protesting that it was business that called him away, he was commanded to stay another two days to see the Queen dance. Melville was obliged to admit that Elizabeth was a more talented dancer than Mary.

Delighted with the praise, Elizabeth sighed again that she wished to meet Mary, if only she could find the time. Melville offered to carry her secretly to Scotland, disguised as a page.

Whilst Melville was waiting for the Queen's official response to his embassy to be drafted by Cecil, he was invited by Leicester to sail back up to London from Hampton Court, in his barge. During the trip, Leicester asked what Mary thought of the proposed marriage. Melville, as instructed by his Queen, answered '*coldly*'. Leicester then hastily assured Melville that he, personally, would never be so presumptuous as to consider himself a suitable husband for Queen Mary. According to Leicester, it was all Cecil's idea, to make Leicester look grasping and ambitious, and disgrace him in the eyes of both queens.

Melville and Leicester dined with the Earl of Pembroke, another Protestant, and brother-in-law to the late Katherine Parr. Pembroke was also a supporter of Mary's rights to the succession. After dinner, Melville took leave of the French and Spanish Ambassadors.

The following day, he received the dispatches from Cecil, together with letters from Cecil to Moray and Lethington. Cecil himself gave Melville a gold chain.

As well as messages from Elizabeth and Cecil, Melville was commissioned to carry other presents. Lady Lennox gave him several items to take as gifts: a diamond ring for Queen Mary; an emerald for own husband; a diamond for Moray; a watch with diamonds and rubies for Lethington and a ruby ring for Melville's brother, Sir Robert Melville. Lady Lennox was courting favour for the idea of marriage of her son, Darnley, to Queen Mary.

Melville arrived back in Edinburgh to report to Mary. In summary, Elizabeth's responses were that she was glad the misunderstanding over the letters was cleared up and that Mary need not fear any action being taken by Parliament to damage her rights without warning.

He could then turn to the messages from others in London. The Spanish Ambassador conveyed the warm wishes of both Philip II, and Philip's son, Don Carlos. Don Carlos was another possible suitor for Mary, but although it was not openly said, Philip did not want him to marry anyone, as he appeared to be mentally unstable.

Mary was pleased that relations with Elizabeth appeared to be mended, but asked Melville if he thought Elizabeth sincere. He replied that he believed not. There had been no 'plain meaning' or 'upright dealing' from Elizabeth but only 'dissimulation'. Melville feared that Elizabeth's intent was to chase Mary out of her own kingdom, as evidenced by the interference in the marriage scheme with Archduke Charles, and the insulting offer of Leicester.

Mary promised Melville she had no intention of marrying Leicester, but sent Moray to meet the Earl of Bedford to talk terms at Berwick – not surprisingly, the English side was not so forthcoming once the match looked like it might take place. Leicester, in the meantime, wrote to Mary, protesting his innocence of any desire to advance himself by marrying her. Mary warmed to Leicester, frightening Elizabeth into thinking the marriage might occur.

It is for this reason, in Melville's view, that Elizabeth allowed Darnley to travel to Scotland – hoping Mary would fall for him. According to Melville, Cecil and Elizabeth did not believe Darnley would disobey Elizabeth's direct orders, for fear of loss of all his lands and titles in England, and the presence of his mother there. They just hoped to muddy the waters and delay Mary marrying anyone.

## Chapter 9: Queen Mary's Friend

Melville was deeply impressed with Mary. He admired her both personally, and as a monarch. On her return from France, she was determined to conduct herself and her kingdom so *'honourably'* and *'discreetly'*, that her good reputation would spread around Europe. She enjoined Melville to advise her, should she make a wrong step. He refused, saying that she had plenty of advisors, including Moray and Lethington. Mary answered that the court was full of flatterers, and she needed someone she could trust to give her honest counsel.

Fearing to trust entirely in princes, Melville was somewhat hesitant, but accepted the Queen's command. From autumn of 1564, he became her chief advisor on foreign affairs – writing most of her letters, and reading everything she received from foreign rulers. He presents the Queen as intelligent and quick-witted, as well as somewhat lonely at the Scottish court, which was smaller and less sophisticated than that of France. Nevertheless, Mary was winning friends both at home and abroad.

Into this happy situation crept the seeds of disaster in the shape of David Rizzio. Rizzio, a Savoyard, became one of Mary's musicians, then her French secretary. His familiarity with the Queen, his Catholic faith, his elegant, foreign ways, and most of all, his contempt for Mary's nobles, created rivalry and animosity. The courtiers would shove him as they passed him in corridors, complaining he was always with the Queen and that he meddled with all of the country's business, rather than just writing letters in French. Instead of keeping out of politics, Rizzio became embroiled as suitors paid him to put forward their pleas to the Queen – this was perfectly normal and not seen as corruption, but there was a limit, and Rizzio, in the view of the Scottish court, overstepped it.

Rizzio, seeing the growing animosity against him, asked Melville's advice. He recommended that Rizzio stand back when the nobles were present, and show them more deference. He then decided that Mary, having asked him to give her advice when she went wrong, would now hear it plain and simple: she should cease favouring Rizzio, and not permit him to be insolent to her Lords.

Mary denied that Rizzio was involved in her business, beyond her French correspondence, but promised to think on Melville's words.

Meanwhile, Lord Darnley was pressing his suit, supported by Melville. Mary turned him down initially, but Darnley persuaded Rizzio to speak in his favour, too. Mary was keen to marry to have an heir, and she was attracted to Darnley. On paper, it was a good match. Darnley was attractive, healthy, well-educated and had a strong claim to the English throne, as well as a moderate claim to the Scottish one. Darnley was widely believed to be a Catholic, although in England he had conformed to the Reformed church established by Elizabeth – again, this should have made him a good choice – Catholic enough for Mary, Protestant enough for her nobles, who were largely of the reformed faith. Eventually, Mary decided to proceed.

Elizabeth sent frantic messages via Sir Nicholas Throckmorton for Darnley to return – or for Mary's nobles to hold out against it until Darnley could be persuaded to confirm allegiance to the Protestant faith.

Mary, angry at further interference in her kingdom, and seeing Elizabeth did not want her to marry at all, ignored the demands to send Darnley back and married him on 29th July, 1565. Her Lords, however, took Elizabeth's money, and broke out into open rebellion – Mary's half-brother, the Earl of Moray, angry at losing his place as her chief advisor; the Duke of Chatelherault, who had been Governor during her childhood, and the Earls of Argyll, Glenrothes and Glencairn concocted a plot to capture Darnley.

Queen Mary dressed herself in armour, and, together with Darnley, now proclaimed as Henry, King of Scots, led her troops in what became known as the *'Chaseabout Raid'*, as the royal army pursued the rebels hither and yon.  The rebels escaped over the border into England, where their failure was greeted by Elizabeth with a refusal to acknowledge any involvement, and a public dressing-down for Moray, in front of the French and Spanish ambassadors.  Moray was forced to confirm Elizabeth's denials, to satisfy France and Spain, who had both accused her of interfering in other kingdoms.

The Scots Lords were concerned that with Mary, Darnley and Rizzio, all Catholics (although, as noted, Darnley (as we will continue to call him that here) was rather flexible in religion) that they would attempt to reconcile Scotland to Rome.  Abroad, the Pope and the Catholic monarchs of Europe had similar ambitions, although Mary had consistently kept her word not to try to overturn the Scottish Reformation.  Pope Pius IV sent Mary 8,000 crowns in furtherance of his hopes, which she never received, as the ship containing it was wrecked on the coast of Northumberland.  Melville was sent to the Earl of Northumberland to ask him to return it, but, despite the Earl (Henry Percy) being a Catholic and, in theory, a supporter of Mary, he hung onto the cash.

## Chapter 10: Marry in Haste

After Mary's marriage, Melville, less needed by the Queen, busy with her new husband, and not liking the growing strife at the Scottish court, requested leave to return to France.  Mary, however, wanted him to stay. She told him that she knew Darnley believed Melville to be a supporter of Moray's but that she herself believed, that, although Melville liked Moray, he was true to her.  She also suggested that he make an effort to get on with Darnley and to continue his friendship with Rizzio.

Melville now advised Mary to forgive Moray and his supporters – they had been badly let down by Elizabeth, and a reconciliation with them would strengthen Mary, as showing herself both powerful enough to defeat rebels, and magnanimous enough to forgive them. Whilst Mary would no doubt have liked to hang them all, there was little she could do, since they were out of her reach in Newcastle, and their families were beginning to talk treason.

This advice was seconded by Sir Nicholas Throckmorton, who suggested that treating Moray and his cohorts mercifully, would encourage English Protestants to look kindly on Mary's claims to the throne, if they saw she could work with their co-religionists. It might persuade those who favoured Lady Katherine Grey as the Protestant heir to change their allegiance to Mary. The Queen, who had shown herself generally as inclined to compromise, listened to their advice, and sent Melville's brother, Sir Robert Melville, to England as her Ambassador, with orders to keep her abreast of any discussions in the English Parliament.

Whilst Melville was encouraging reconciliation, Mary received a letter from her brother-in-law, Charles IX, urging her, on the advice of her uncle, the Cardinal of Lorraine, to have nothing to do with her Protestant rebels. The Cardinal was fresh from the Council of Trent, where the Catholic powers of Europe had pledged themselves to root out Protestantism. Mary was in a quandary – she did not wish to offend her family, or the powerful kings of France or Spain, but she had accepted the wisdom of Throckmorton and Melville's advice, and they both knew more of events in England than Charles or Philip.

After some deliberation, Mary continued with the Parliament that had been originally called to forfeit the goods and titles of Moray and his colleagues. Meanwhile, another plot was brewing.

James Douglas, Earl of Morton; his cousin Sir George Douglas, who was Darnley's illegitimate uncle; Patrick, Lord Ruthven (Douglas' brother-in-law) and Patrick, Lord Lindsay (Moray's brother-in-law) now banded together to dispose of the hated David Rizzio. They persuaded Darnley to join with them, playing on the fact that, within a very short space of time after their marriage, Mary had lost all respect for him, and refused to grant him the Crown Matrimonial (ie, the right to remain king should she die with an underage heir, or, if she had no heir, for the crown to pass to him). Darnley was jealous of Rizzio, suspecting he had undermined him to Mary. There is also a theory that Rizzio and Darnley had been lovers.

The plotters burst into Mary's supper chamber at Holyrood Palace, held her fast (although she was six months' pregnant) and stabbed Rizzio to death. Mary was then locked into her room.

Melville claims that, the next day, he came into the gates of the Palace, and Mary called to him from a window for help, telling him to fetch the Provost of Edinburgh, and raise troops to rescue her. As he tried to leave the Palace, he encountered James Nesbit, one of the Earl of Lennox' men, and persuaded him that he, Melville, was only going to hear the preaching in St Giles Kirk, it being a Sunday. Instead, he hurried to the Provost, but the citizens of Edinburgh declined to involve themselves.

Mary smuggled out another message to Melville to give to Moray, guessing that her half-brother would return immediately. She was right, for he appeared in Edinburgh on the Monday - which suggests he was aware of the plot, as he had been in Newcastle - a distance of 120 miles, which could hardly be done in less than a day. Her message to Moray was that she knew she would not have been so badly treated, had he been there, and that, if he helped her now, she would forgive his previous rebellion.

The Queen turned her undoubted charm on her husband, and, in a show of quick thinking and resolution it is hard not to admire, persuaded him that he should abandon his co-conspirators, who only meant to harm them both.

He realised she was right, and the pair of them came up with a scheme to enable them to escape from Edinburgh and ride as hard as they could for Dunbar Castle. Messages were left with Melville for Moray, and further messengers sent from Dunbar to the lords in exile in Newcastle to return. Their doings were as nothing in Mary's eyes, compared with the slaughter of her servant in her presence – a proceeding that was surely intended to cause her to miscarry, and perhaps die. If murdering Rizzio were their only goal, Morton and his allies could have done it anywhere.

Moray, who was not, perhaps, as ruthless as some of his fellow nobles, was overcome with remorse when he saw Mary, who kissed and hugged him. He promised to have nothing to do with Morton and his crew.

### Chapter 11: Reconciliation?

Melville was delighted that Mary and Moray were reconciled, and tried to persuade her to forgive Darnley, casting the blame on George Douglas for leading him astray – but his words fell on deaf ears. The Queen had nothing but a '*great grudge*' in her heart against her husband. Darnley, failing to understand that he was now in a dangerous position, then worked himself up, complaining to Melville because Moray had written only to Mary, not recognising him as king.

Darnley enquired as to the whereabouts of Morton and the rest, to which Melville replied that he had no idea. The King's answer was brusque – '*as they have brewed, so let them drink*,' but Melville believed that Darnley regretted abandoning them. Her purpose won, Mary was being extremely cold. Hardly surprising, one might think, when her husband conspired against her, killed her friend in her presence, and allowed men to mishandle her – Ruthven even pointing a gun at her pregnant belly.

Melville tried to patch things up – he seems to have thought better of Darnley than did most others of his acquaintance – saying his folly was due to poor advice, and inexperience rather than ill-will. Mary became so fed up with Melville's support of Darnley that Moray was dispatched to tell him to cease his interference.

A new character now enters centre-stage in the Scottish court, James Hepburn, Earl of Bothwell. Bothwell was one of the few Scots lords who had never been paid by either France or England, and it appeared that, together with his confederates, the Earl of Huntly, and the Bishop of Ross, he was unhappy that Moray had been received back into favour. Mary was reverting to the advice that Melville and Throckmorton had given – to court Moray to appease the Protestant faction in England, but Bothwell suggested that Moray should be held under house arrest while Mary was in childbed, to prevent him inviting Morton and the other banished lords back home.

Melville claims to have dissuaded her from this notion, but his own position was awkward. His brother, Sir Robert, who was now Ambassador to Elizabeth, had been asking the English government to send Morton out of England. At the same time, Melville's sister, Margaret, who was married to Morton's relative, Sir John Johnstone of Elphinstone, asked her brother to write to the Elector Palatine, to give Morton refuge. Melville showed the letters to the Queen, and discussed both Moray and Morton with her. She decided not to put Moray under arrest, but Melville was forbidden to do anything to help Morton.

A new Ambassador came from England, none other than the Henry Killigrew who had helped Melville following the Battle of St Quentin. At this point in his memoirs, Melville only mentions that Killigrew was an old friend, who had been known to him in France. He does not mention a warmer relationship, however, a couple of letters from both Melville and his brother Robert, suggest that the acquaintanceship was in fact, very close. Killigrew's wife, Katherine Cooke, was the sister of Mildred Cooke, who was wife to Sir William Cecil, Elizabeth's Secretary of State. Killigrew had been at the heart of English diplomacy since Elizabeth's accession.

Killigrew was to confirm to Mary that Morton and the others had been sent publicly out of England (although, in fact, they were there in hiding, to the English government's knowledge). He was also to congratulate Mary on her escape from the rebels, but was to question her about her dealings with the Irish chieftain, O'Neill.

The English government had also sent a spy, one Rokeby, who claimed to be a Catholic and a supporter of Mary's right to the English succession. The plan was for him to worm his way into Mary's confidence and report back to Cecil on her plans. Melville's brother got wind of the plot and warned Melville and Mary, so that when Ambassador Killigrew huffed and puffed about Mary entertaining Rokeby, a rebellious English subject, Mary immediately had the spy arrested and all his papers taken, amongst which were found letters from Cecil.

Rokeby was clapped into prison, and Mary, continuing to hide her knowledge that he was a spy, told Killigrew that he had been apprehended to please Elizabeth, who could have him delivered to her custody as soon as she liked.

Anticipating the birth of her child, Mary again prepared to send Melville to England, drafting letters lacking only the information on the child's gender, and requesting Elizabeth to send suitable god-parents, to promote friendship between them.

## Chapter 12: England Again

Melville waited in Edinburgh Castle, praying for Mary to bear a healthy son.  Between ten and eleven in the morning of 19ᵗʰ June, 1566, the Queen's lady-in-waiting, Lady Boyd, came with the good news that mother and son were doing well.  Melville set out for London, reaching Berwick by nightfall, and London on the fourth day.  He went first to his brother, then to Cecil, but asked them to keep it secret until he was in Elizabeth's presence.  He travelled with Cecil to Greenwich, where Elizabeth was dancing after supper.  Cecil whispered in her ear.  Silence fell.  The Queen put her hands to her head and sank onto a cushion, saying:

*'the Queen of Scots [was] lighter of a fair son, whilst [she was] but a barren stock.'*

The next morning, the Melville brothers were sent for.  They were privately told that Elizabeth was deeply depressed by the news, but had been advised to put a good face on it, which she immediately proceeded to do, telling them the news had cheered her immensely, after a fortnight of illness.

Melville told Elizabeth that the news had been sent first to her, as Mary knew she would rejoice.  He added, off his own bat, that although she was delighted to have a son, Mary had been so badly treated, that she wished she had never married.  Elizabeth was once again toying with the idea of matrimony, so Melville was keen to discourage her.

Elizabeth accepted the invitation to stand godmother.  It would be a good opportunity, he said, for the queens to meet.  Alas, however, although Elizabeth was eager to meet her *'dear sister'*, affairs would not permit her to travel.  She would send proxies.

Melville then reported on Killigrew, explaining his long stay in Scotland by his waiting for Mary to give birth.  He thanked the Queen on

Mary's behalf for sending Morton and the others out of the country – he did not believe the rumours that they were being hidden – surely none of her subjects could be so disobedient! Indeed not, returned Elizabeth. If such a thing transpired to be true, severe punishment would follow. He also offered to send the alleged criminal Rokeby back, but Elizabeth seemingly forgot to ask him to arrange it.

It appeared to Melville that Leicester, Pembroke and the Duke of Norfolk were even more supportive of Mary being named heir, now that she had a son. Only Cecil seemed to have doubts. Melville assured Elizabeth that Mary would not dream of pushing herself forward into Elizabeth's shoes, she only wished to be named as successor.

The birth of the Prince, the Queen returned smoothly, just made it more urgent for the English lawyers to determine the legal position. When Melville pointed out that she had made the same point a year before, she told him that the proxies she would send for the christening would tell Mary more. He clearly was not going to receive confirmation of Mary's position, so Melville returned to Scotland, leaving his brother behind, but the richer by a chain from the Queen.

He found Mary depressed and with a poor appetite – not recovered from the events surrounding the murder of Rizzio, and the threat to her life. Melville tried to cheer her, assuring her of many friends in both Scotland and England. He also suggested that forgiving Morton and the others would be a good move. Mary promised to think on the matter, and began to talk of allowing the rebels to be restored. Bothwell, getting wind of this, began to commune with them secretly.

The Earl of Bedford and the French and Spanish Ambassadors were to come to Stirling for the christening and Melville was sent to meet the Earl at Coldingham. Bedford was accompanied by a large group of English lords and gentlemen, including Master Carey, son of Elizabeth's cousin, Lord Hunsdon, and Sir Christopher Hatton, who, although a great friend of Elizabeth, was widely believed to be a Catholic, and a supporter of Mary's.

The English representatives were well treated, but were somewhat shocked at the little account paid to Darnley. They told Melville to advise Mary to treat him more respectfully, as it reflected badly on her to be at odds with her husband.

Mary began to recover her spirits, and rode to the Border to give justice in person, as her father, James V, and grandfather, James IV, had done. Bothwell and Huntly were both with her, and, according to Melville, tried to plot the death of Moray, but were prevented by Lord Home.

The Queen rode as far as Berwick, now in English hands, and was greeted with an artillery display. The Warden of Berwick, Sir John Foster, came to meet her, to discuss peace-keeping. Whether his horse was frightened by the noise or for some other reason, it reared up, and tried to bite the Queen's horse in the neck, before striking Mary a severe blow on the thigh with a front hoof. The mortified Sir John leapt off his horse and fell to the ground, begging pardon. Mary graciously told him that she was not hurt, but was obliged to stay at Castle Home for two days.

Bothwell was riding high – he persuaded Mary to allow Morton to return. Mary then set about trying to reconcile Bothwell, Huntly, Argyll and Moray, and was successful, at least on the surface.

### Chapter 13: The Murder of Darnley

Whilst Mary was in the Borders, Darnley followed her about miserably, but received short shrift. He retired to Glasgow, where he fell ill. On partial recovery, he moved to a house at Kirk O'Fields, where

Mary visited him, and the two appeared to be moving towards a reconciliation.

According to Melville himself, although he was writing with hindsight and we should be careful of being wise after the event, there were rumours current in Edinburgh that Bothwell meant to harm Darnley. So when the King was found dead in the garden of his house, following an explosion, the finger of suspicion was immediately pointed at the Earl.

Melville went to the Queen, but was told by Bothwell that she was too upset to see anyone. In the meantime, Melville could look at Darnley's body, which had not suffered a mark – he had actually escaped from the house before the explosion, and, it was presumed, had been suffocated. Melville reports that he could not actually get a sight of the corpse, which was being guarded by one Alexander Durem.

Then an even more damaging rumour began to circulate – that Bothwell (a Protestant), recently married to the Catholic Lady Jean Gordon, sister of the Earl of Huntley, would divorce Lady Jean to marry the Queen. Mary's nobles were shocked and appalled at the dishonour this would bring on their Queen. One of them, Sir John Maxwell, 4th Lord Herries, and a Protestant himself, went on his knees to Mary to beg her to put any idea of marrying Bothwell out of her mind. Mary assured Herries that she had no such intent.

Melville, planning to second Herries' plea, received a letter from a man named Thomas Bishop. Bishop was a Scot, and had been for a long time in the service of the Earl of Lennox, with whose wife he quarrelled bitterly. From information that Melville could not have known, it seems likely that Bishop was also in the pay of Sir William Cecil, and Leicester at different times.

Bishop's story is so convoluted that it is hard to know whose side he was on, but Melville obviously took him at face value. Bishop wrote that England was full of rumours that Mary was to marry Bothwell, believed to be Darnley's murderer, and advised Melville to warn her strongly that such an action would lead to her downfall.

Melville took the letter to the Queen, who read it, and returned it. She then called Lethington over to read it, and told him that the letter was a ploy of Melville's own, to ruin Bothwell. Lethington took Melville aside, and, having read the letter, warned him to leave Edinburgh, as Bothwell would kill him.

When Bothwell returned, Mary informed him of the letter, asking him to leave Melville alone, but Melville, fearing Lethington was true in his estimate of Bothwell's character, went into hiding until Mary was able to persuade Bothwell to cease threatening him. Apparently, the Queen told Bothwell that he would leave her with no friends at all. Melville then returned to her side, telling her the letter truly had come from Bishop, but even if he had made it up, she should still listen to advice from those who wished her well. Mary again denied planning to marry Bothwell, but would not be drawn far into the topic.

A few days later, Mary travelled to Stirling to see her baby, Prince James, and on her return journey, she, together with Melville, the Earl of Huntly and Lethington, were abducted by Bothwell and his henchman, Captain Blackater, and carried off to Dunbar. Blackater told Melville that the Queen was party to the abduction, but that has been disputed.

Melville was allowed to leave Dunbar – presumably Bothwell did not want anyone stiffening any resolve Mary might have to resist him. During this period Bothwell and Mary slept together – whether he forced her has been a bone of contention for 450 years.

Bothwell persuaded a portion of the nobility to petition Mary to marry him. He divorced his wife and the pair were married on 15th May 1567. Mary was still only 24 years old – she had lost two husbands, been abducted and perhaps raped. Nowadays, we might think that she had fallen into the common syndrome of putting all her trust in the man who was abusing her. For her subjects, however, her actions were seen as adulterous, dishonourable and demeaning to her position.

Melville had avoided the court since he had been released from Dunbar, but was present at the marriage. Here, we find a small slice of the man's own appearance and personality. Bothwell said that Melville had been quite the stranger – he should sit down and dine with him. Melville replied shortly that he had already eaten. Well, then they should drink together, came the reply, as Bothwell thrust a cup of wine on Melville for them to toast each other, like, as Melville says contemptuously, 'Dutchmen'. Melville merely sipped at the wine. Bothwell told him to drink up, until he put some weight on, for 'the zeal of the common weal has eaten you up and made you so lean.' Melville replied that, whilst he should try to be useful, it was up to Bothwell and the nobles to consider the public good. Bothwell then started to talk of women, 'speaking such filthy language' that Melville hurried away, a small outpost of sober dutifulness amidst a sea of self-serving brutes.

He went to the Queen, who was, unsurprisingly, glad to see him. Ever since she had returned to Scotland, she had tried to inculcate a more cultured and sophisticated court, but all her work was undone.

## Chapter 14: Queen Mary's Downfall

Melville now became concerned as to the fate of Mary's son, Prince James. The child was in the keeping of the Earl of Mar, at Stirling, but Bothwell, apparently, was trying to get the child into his own hands and Mar was worried that once the Prince was in Bothwell's power, he would not make old bones.

Melville was unable to help directly, but aware that Sir James Balfour, who was the Keeper of Edinburgh Castle, and a former crony of Bothwell's, had quarrelled with him and refused to take part in the murder of Darnley, Melville went to Balfour, and told him to hold on to the castle. By so doing he might be able to help both Prince James and Queen Mary, who was now in such a state of despair that she was threatening to harm herself. If Balfour handed over the castle, he would be pursued with Bothwell for the murder of the late King.

For that faction of the nobility who were not supporters of Bothwell, were now hoping to pursue him for the murder, and planned to crown James as King. Bothwell was warned that a march on Holyrood was planned, so he left abruptly, taking Mary with him, and raced for Dunbar.

Melville had been a faithful supporter of Mary during her active reign, but once Bothwell was in the picture, his allegiance to Moray came to the fore. Moray and the Lords raised an army, and so did Bothwell and the Queen. The forces met at Carberry Hill on 15th June 1567. Many in Bothwell's army believed that Mary was secretly in league with Lords, because he had treated her so badly. From the events, this appears to be true. No battle was fought, but negotiations resulted in Mary leaving her army and returning to Edinburgh with the Lords.

This should have been a liberation for her, but she had been double-crossed again, the Lords had no intention of allowing her to resume power. She was shouted at and insulted in the streets as a whore and a murderer.

It has been pointed out, by Robert Stedall in his 'The Challenge to the Crown: The Struggle for Supremacy in the Reign of Mary, Queen of Scots' that one of the reasons the Lords were eager to replace Mary with another minor was financial. Under Scots law, when a sovereign reached the age of twenty-five, he or she could resume all lands that had been granted away during his or her minority. Mary would be twenty-five in the forthcoming December, and, as the Crown was in a poor financial state would be very likely to do so. Another long minority would allow the nobility to continue to help themselves to Crown lands.

Whether their reasons were financial, religious or political, Mary was imprisoned at Lochleven. Whilst there, she was bullied into abdicating, having been assured, by Melville's brother, who remained one of her staunchest supporters, that anything done under duress could not be binding. Still trusting her brother, Moray, most of all the lords, she requested he be appointed as Regent.

There were now two parties in Scotland – the Queen's Party, that believed she had abdicated under duress, and the King's Party, who wished for a Regency. Melville seems to have equivocated somewhat. Initially, there was no open rupture, and Melville was sent to Berwick to meet Moray (who had been in France, avoiding both the death of Darnley, and its aftermath). Melville also had a commission from those in the King's Party who had only wished for the overthrow of Bothwell, and not for the deposition of Mary, to encourage Moray to make terms with the Queen that would bring her back to power, guided by him.

Moray, after some pressing, accepted the Regency, but when he went to Mary in Lochleven they quarrelled so bitterly (because, according to Melville he used *'language to break her heart')* that *'it cut the thread of credit and love between the Queen and [Moray] for ever.'*

In the meantime, as Melville notes, the English did all they could to *'kindle the fire'*, promising support to both sides, sending embassies under Throckmorton, Drury, Randolph, Davison and others. Apparently Throckmorton was so disgusted by the double-dealing of his own colleagues that he leaked information to Melville.

Mary then escaped from Lochleven Castle and supported by a good number of the nobles, took up arms. According to Melville, this all happened too soon – that Moray, over time, would have softened his stance and restored her. The Queen however, was pushed into giving battle early – she would have preferred to make a base at Dumbarton

Castle and gather support gradually, but the Hamiltons, who were her chief supporters, were keen for battle.

At Langside on 13th May 1568, the Queen's forces were defeated, and she lost courage, which, Melville comments, she had never done before. Mary fled to England, and was never permitted her freedom again.

## Chapter 15: Melville's Marriage

A commission was convened by Queen Elizabeth at York in October 1568 to look into whether Mary had been involved in the death of Darnley. Moray and others of the King's Party were present, including Melville and his adoptive father, Henry Balnaves. The Commission was then moved to Hampton Court. The results were inconclusive, as Elizabeth had no intention of allowing Mary to be either convicted or cleared.

On his return to Scotland following the Commission, Melville got married for the first time, or so it appears. On 29th June 1569, a deed was presented before the Lords of Session, of whom Balnaves was one, to be registered. Dated both Balmuto and Edinburgh, the deed provided for the marriage of James Melville, adopted son of Balnaves, to marry Christian Boswell, daughter of Sir David Boswell of Balmuto.

It seems likely that the Boswells were connections of Balnaves' wife, who left £12 for the dowry of Helen Boswell in her will, although the relationship between Helen and Christian is unknown. There is no information as to whether Melville and Christian had any say in the matter of their marriage. They went on to have four children, two boys and two girls. In February of the following year, Balnaves died, and Melville inherited his lands at Halhill.

No mention is made of any other wife, before or after, however, a letter in the Cecil Papers at Hatfield gives a startling idea that Melville was at some point married to the sister of Henry Killigrew.

In June 1560, there is a letter addressed from Melville to Killigrew, in which he refers to him as *'his gentle brother'*. It is possible that the two men were so close they called each other brother (although that doesn't seem to have been a common practice) or, that Melville was married to Killigrew's sister, but that she died before he married Christian Boswell. However, there is a later letter of Melville's dated 7th December, 1583, also addressing Killigrew as *'brother'*, and, in the post-script, adding,

*'Your sister my wyf [wife] has hir hartly recommendit unto zow [you]'* that is, your sister, my wife, sends her hearty recommendations to you.

There are also letters in which Melville's brother, Robert, refers to Killigrew as brother.

So, it is a mystery – was Melville married twice? If so, which was the first wife? Or did the marriage to Christian never take place? But, if Melville were already married, why would Balnaves try to arrange a marriage to Christian? Further, if Melville had kept a marriage to Miss Killigrew secret, he would have had to confess it rather than commit bigamy with Christian. It would be surprising if such a confession resulted in a bequest to Melville's wife in the will Balnaves made less than six months after the bond to marry Christian.

It is a mystery, which our research has not yet solved!

## Chapter 16: Regencies of Moray and Lennox.

Moray's Regency began to degenerate into faction, and quarrels. Melville, a firm supporter of Moray, tried to advise him, but his opinion of the Regent was that he was *'good with good company, wise with wise company, stout with stout company, and contrariwise with others of contrary qualities.'*

The Regent was assassinated by a member of the Hamilton family (who were of the Queen's Party) in January 1570. In his stead, the Earl of Lennox, grandfather to King James, was suggested as Regent. At the same time, the Earl of Sussex was approaching the border with a large army. Melville was sent by a group who, whilst part of the King's Party, were sympathetic to the Queen, to see what Sussex' intentions were.

Melville was greeted courteously and even lent the Earl's own furred nightgown (not a sleeping garment, more like an informal evening coat) as a token of how welcome he was. Sussex was full of gracious words – he respected the Queen of Scots, and her son, whom he took to be his own Queen's next heirs; he was not planning to assist either side or involve himself in Scotland's internal affairs. He was, in fact, just following orders.

Melville left the English camp, convinced that Sussex was, in truth, there to support the installation of Lennox as Regent and to promise assistance to the King's Party, whilst also sending messages of support to the Queen's Party, thus to foment further strife in Scotland. The Lennox and Hamilton families had been enemies for generations, so the appointment of Lennox as Regent would certainly limit any chance of reconciliation between the two sides.

Sussex crossed the border and took two castles, one of which was Home, driving Lord Home into the Queen's Party.

Melville, who had been a supporter of the Darnley marriage, was on good terms with Lennox, and went to visit him. Lennox told Melville that Lady Lennox had recommended that he listen to advice from both Melville and his brother. The best advice that Melville could give was for Lennox to refuse the Regency, as it would probably cost him his life. He warned Lennox that he would have enemies (including a small group, originally in the King's Party, but alienated by Moray, who were now holding Edinburgh Castle for the Queen).  Melville promised to serve Lennox as Regent.

One of Lennox' first actions was to capture a castle in the hands of the Queen's Party.  Melville had planned to ride with him, in part because he had been promised lands at Monimail, formerly in the possession of the Bishop of St Andrews, and then owned by Henry Balnaves.  He was persuaded to stay in Edinburgh by the English ambassador, Sir Thomas Randolph, to try to broker a peace with the members of the Queen's Party, still holding out in Edinburgh Castle.  Randolph said he would speak to Lennox about the lands, making sure they were given to Melville.

Melville now claims to have been hoodwinked by Randolph.  He believed Randolph to be his friend, as he had helped him during Randolph's exile in France during the reign of Mary I of England. Randolph told Melville that he himself believed (in his personal capacity, not as Ambassador) that the only true authority in Scotland was Mary, and so Melville became a go-between Randolph and Sir William Kirkcaldy of Grange, who was holding the castle.

Kirkcaldy had originally been one of the King's Party, but was increasingly disaffected, and after Moray's death, had changed sides. Kirkcaldy and Melville had been friends for many years.  In Melville's view, Kirkcaldy was still open to reconciliation with Lennox, as he believed that internal strife in Scotland was just giving more opportunity to England to stir up trouble.

Randolph suggested that Kirkcaldy surrender the castle to an English appointee, at which point Kirkcaldy refused to have any further discussions.  His position hardened, and he refused to give up the castle to the King's Party.

Melville quarrelled with Randolph, probably because he failed to obtain the promised lands for him – even supporting their grant elsewhere. He now saw, or so he says, that Randolph had only meant to sow dissension.

There are two letters, written a fortnight apart in March 1572 from Melville to Randolph. In the first he talks of their old friendship and says he prefers to stay quietly in the country and not involve himself in affairs. In the second, he addresses him in very stiff language, requesting him to desist from harrying Melville's widowed mother, who feared that Randolph would burn her property in revenge for attacks upon Morton.

## Chapter 17: Regencies of Mar and Morton

Lennox had a rival for the Regency, in the Earl of Morton, and within the King's Party there were supporters of both. Melville, continuing in his support for Lennox, because, he says, there was no point in hoping for the Queen to be freed, was taken into custody by the Earl of Buchan, with a threat to try him for some unspecified crime. The purpose, apparently, was to use him as a hostage to persuade Kirkcaldy to surrender Edinburgh Castle. Melville pointed out that the Castle group were so angry with him, that this plan could never work.

Nevertheless, Kirkcaldy obviously did retain some affection for him as he sent a secret message to Melville with an escape plan. Melville rejected the offer, saying he knew Buchan would not harm him, and he was eventually freed.

Melville gives his reasons for supporting the King's Party, as that he could see no hope for Mary to ever be freed – the English government would never let her go, and although the French might complain, they would not help. Catherine de Medici did not like her former daughter-in-law and, from the French perspective, the uniting of England and

Scotland under a single monarch would be a poor proposition. Mary's relatives, the Guises, had never done more than use her for their own advantage. Spain too, would not help Mary, as it had enough to do with its problems in controlling Flanders.

Kirkcaldy now came up with a plan that, he hoped, would reconcile the two parties. The King's Party were planning to hold a Parliament at Stirling, so Kirkcaldy sent for as many as possible of the Queen's Party to surprise the others at Stirling, and take control of the Regent and his government, so an agreement could be worked out. Inevitably, matters went awry, and Lennox was shot, despite it having been agreed beforehand that there would be no violence. Kirkcaldy was beside himself as any hope of concord now disappeared.

Randolph pushed forward the Earl of Morton as Regent – Morton being decidedly pro-English, but the King's Party preferred the Earl of Mar. Whilst there was not open warfare, there were endless skirmishes between the groups.

Mar retired to Stirling, and Randolph, now hated by both sides, returned to England. Henry Killigrew, who had been on previous embassies, and had once been Melville's friend, now returned as ambassador. He was charged, he told Melville, with promoting peace – although the Queen of England favoured the Queen's Party. Melville then rounded on his former friend, saying that he knew that Killigrew was only in Scotland to make more trouble, and that as fellow-Protestants the English ministers should be ashamed of themselves for encouraging discord. Killigrew had to admit that his real intention was to see Morton installed as Regent.

Regent Mar sent for Melville to act yet again as go-between with the Queen's Party. Mar seems to have been an honest man, desperate for peace and reconciliation in Scotland. Melville was to ask Kirkcaldy for terms for surrender of the Castle. Kirkcaldy said that he would not sell himself for profit, but that his party would come to terms and support the Regent for so long as the Queen was detained in England, and that, should she be freed, he was sure she and her son could be reconciled.

Mar and Kirkcaldy came to terms, but, before their agreement could be shared with the rest of the King's Party, Mar died. He had recently dined with Morton, and there were suggestions of poison, but it was probably natural.

Morton then summoned Melville and persuaded him that he would fulfil the agreement made by Mar, to finally bring an end to the civil strife. He wanted to make peace with all of the Queen's Party, he said, and Kircaldy would be suitably rewarded. So Melville went back to Kirkcaldy, and persuaded him that he should surrender. Kirkcaldy agreed, on the proviso that Huntly and the Hamiltons, who were Mary's strongest adherents, but not involved in the holding of the Castle, should be included in the general peace. He refused to receive any sweeteners himself.

Morton did not like this – he had no intention of coming to terms with the rich Huntly and Hamilton families – there would be no profit in that! He just wanted reconciliation with the relatively poor Kirkcaldy.

Kirkcaldy was shocked, telling Melville it would disgrace him to abandon Huntly and the Hamiltons (who all along would have been happy to be reconciled with the King's Party.) He would prefer that they should betray him, than that he himself should act dishonourably. Nevertheless, he would surrender the Castle if the rest of the Queen's Party were included in discussion.

Melville carried this message back and agreed with Morton that the Castle would be surrendered in six months' time, once Morton had shown he intended to keep faith. This was agreed to and Morton then sent messages to Huntly and the Hamiltons who agreed terms.

Immediately he had half of the Queen's Party on side Morton proclaimed that Kirkcaldy and the others in the Castle were traitors and had refused to come to reasonable terms. Morton collected English troops to besiege the Castle, and, owing to the dry summer, Kirkcaldy was obliged to surrender as the wells ran dry. Among the men in the castle were two of Melville's brothers.

It was agreed with Kirkcaldy that he and his colleagues would be brought into the King's Peace, and their lands restored, but after three days of liberty, during which time they stayed with the English Warden of Berwick, a letter was received from Queen Elizabeth, ordering the Warden to hand over the men to Morton. Melville's brother's life was spared, on petition from Killigrew. Lord Home was spared but died soon after, but Kirkcaldy, who could claim to be the only honourable man in Scotland, was hanged on 3rd August 1573.

Morton, having disposed of all of his rivals, and supported by the English, proved an effective Regent, although there were many who disliked him, and believed him to be an extortioner.

### Chapter 18: Childhood of James VI

Melville seems to have taken a step back from public affairs at this point, although where he was, and how he passed is time, is unknown. Presumably, he was at Halhill with his wife, bringing up a young family.

He recounts how the young King, James, was brought up at Stirling by Lady Mar, and the Lord Erskine, neither of whom were friends to Morton. Morton was forced to resign in 1578 when James was twelve, but attempted to regain power in 1579. In 1580, he was publicly accused of murdering Darnley, and arrested. The English, displeased by the overthrow of their preferred Regent, made warlike noises, but James and his advisors (his cousin, Esme Stuart, Duke of Lennox, who was nephew of the assassinated Regent Lennox, and Lord James Stewart, Earl of Arran) raised taxation for an army, and the English retreated – not so enamoured of Morton that they wished to go to war.

The young King's favouring of Lennox and Arran was not popular with his other lords, and a scheme was hatched to deal with them. Lennox had converted to the Presbyterian faith that was now the official religion of Scotland, but his conversion was considered suspect.

In 1582, Melville reappears at the forefront of affairs. He had been appointed a Justice in Ayre in West Lothian. One morning, an unknown man came into his bedroom with a story of a plot against Lennox, Arran and the King. Melville warned Lennox, but it was too late. James had been captured and was being held at Stirling Castle by a group who became known as the Lords Enterprisers.

Both Queen Elizabeth and King Henri III of France sent messages to James, assuring him they would help him escape, but James, aged sixteen, was too wise to fall into the trap of accepting foreign aid. He was very happy in the care of his subjects, he said, who had mistakenly thought ill of the Duke of Lennox and Earl of Arran.

James, however, was just biding his time. He called a meeting of his nobles at St Andrew's, ostensibly to hear the report of two ambassadors he had sent to England. He summoned to it all of the Lords who had not been involved in his detention, including Melville. Melville was loath to attend – he was tired of public life, and the strife and factions he had seen in his many years of service, and had hoped to continue a quiet life in retirement. He was now in his late forties – not considered very old by the standards of the day, but certainly not young.

However, duty called, and he trundled off to James at Falkland, where he listened to James complaining about how badly he had been treated. Melville pointed out that minorities were always difficult times, with factions and self-seeking abounding but that the best thing for a King to do on attaining his majority, was to forget the past. James, not entirely taking Melville's advice, rode on to St Andrew's having made a proclamation that only such lords as he had sent for should meet him there. Melville was angry, believing that the Lords Enterprisers would ignore the orders and come to St Andrew's quicker than the ones sent for. His misgivings were proven correct as uninvited lords and their retinues turned up.

James however, persuaded them that he would let bygones be bygones, and that he bore no grudge for his imprisonment. He then called Melville up before the whole court, and praised him for his good advice –much to Melville's embarrassment, and also annoyance, as he was already disliked for having given the King warning of the plot against him.

In due course, James' friend, the Earl of Arran, petitioned to be allowed back to court. James asked Melville's advice and received the answer that for him to hide the truth would imperil James, but to tell it would imperil Melville. On being asked to explain, Melville told James that Arran was a trouble maker, and that if he were returned to favour, factions would break out again. If Arran found out that he had advised James against returning him to favour, Melville's life would be endangered.

James decided that Arran should be allowed back to court once, so that his other lords could see that Arran should be well-treated, but that Arran should then retire. Arran, however, refused to leave and soon regained the King's ear. In Melville's opinion, things went from bad to worse as Arran prevented the King from hearing other advice.

Melville was not the only one to advise James to be rid of Arran. Elizabeth wrote, reprimanding him for going back on his promise to treat all his lords equally. Melville was deputed to draft an answer, which was along the lines of telling Elizabeth to mind her own business.

Arran now had considerable influence, and, as Melville had predicted, wanted to get him out of the way. He suggested that Melville be sent on an embassy to England. Melville was summoned to Stirling, where he handed the King a long letter, full of advice on good governance. On being told of the plan to send him to England, Melville told the King that the English would never respect James and consider him as the heir to the English Crown until he had got his own house in order, and that it was not the right time for an embassy. James accepted the advice and allowed Melville to return home.

### Chapter 19: Breach with Arran

Elizabeth had followed up her letter of admonition with an ambassador who proved to be none other than that Puritan enemy of Mary, Queen of Scots, Sir Francis Walsingham. Melville, who had known Walsingham for many years, was sent to meet him and bring him to James.

Walsingham met the King, and claimed to be very impressed with him, but refused to have anything to do with Arran, who got his revenge by substituting a diamond ring sent to Walsingham from the King with a glass one.

James suggested that Melville might become his Secretary, but Melville refused. Melville and Arran quarrelled in Council, when Arran shouted that Melville's love for the Lords Enterprisers would ruin the King. Melville replied smartly that Arran's love for their lands would do the job. This open breach eventuated in Melville being removed from the Council, with the excuse from James that it would be unsuitable to have two brothers on the Council (Sir Robert Melville had been a Councillor for many years). Nevertheless, James added, when he married, Melville would be appointed as Councillor to his Queen.

Glad to be relieved of involvement in a government he feared was heading for disaster, Melville consented to go to England again, and an obsequious letter to Elizabeth was penned. Before he could depart, Melville again took James to task about favouring the Earl of Arran, who, he said was undermining James' promise to forgive the Lords Enterprisers. Arran demanded to know why Melville was undermining him, and asked who he thought should be around the King instead?

The two men lost their tempers, and Arran swore that he would kill Melville if he *fished in his waters* again. Melville shouted back that he would find more honest men to protect him than Arran would find throat-cutters to kill him.

James, angry at such a scene, sent a rebuke to Arran, who retired in a sulk to Edinburgh Castle, not returning until Melville left the court, believing the King did not want him to remain. The mission to England was dropped.

So James' reign continued, with continual strife between Arran and the other lords, culminating in the execution of the Earl of Gowrie, Arran's particular bete noir.

Another embassy arrived from London, led by William Davison, which had orders this time to deal with Arran. Melville again believed that the English were just plotting to keep the factions alive in Scotland, especially as Arran was persuaded to prevent James marrying for at least three years.

The English Council had yet another trick up its sleeve. They sent a new Ambassador, named Wootton, who was to be the King's friend and to spend time with him hunting and in other pastimes. Melville had met Wootton thirty years before, at the French Court, when he had tried to trick the Constable, Montmorency, into breaking the peace with England. Melville did not trust him and warned James to beware. James however, took to Wootton.

Melville was proved right. It was time for James to look for a wife, and a Danish Embassy arrived to begin negotiations. According to Melville, Arran and Wootton between them did everything they could to undermine negotiations and the Danish ambassadors were mistreated and insulted.

Melville explained to the offended Danes that, although the Queen of England was a '*wise princess*' there were many about her who did not wish James to be her successor, and so were making every effort to prevent James forming alliances or marrying. He then informed James of the insults that the Danes were receiving and persuaded him to treat them well.

Arran was about to get his come-uppance. A disturbance on the Border resulted in a murder, for which he was held responsible, and imprisoned. After a few days he was released, but commanded to return to his own lands.

## Chapter 20: Last Years of Service

Further uprisings and plots occurred in the 1580s, and eventually Arran was completely dismissed, as James took more power into his own hands. Melville remained a member of the Privy Council but began to withdraw from affairs. Several embassies were proposed for Melville – to England, to Spain, to Denmark and even to Navarre but he refused them all, preferring to retire to his lands at Halhill. Nevertheless, he continued to correspond with both Scottish and English lords, including Archibald Douglas, 8th Earl of Angus, whom he thanked in 1588 for sending a pair of virginals as a gift for Melville's daughter.

He even refused a final embassy to Denmark, to treat of the King's marriage to Anne of Denmark – suggesting his brother be sent instead.

On the arrival of the Queen Anne, Melville was summoned back to court to meet her. He was knighted at her coronation on 17th May, 1590 and was appointed to her Council, where he served for some years. Initially, the Queen did not like him, but she warmed to him over time.

During the 1590s more plots and attempts to control James were discovered, and it is with an air of weariness that Melville recounts the endless shufflings for favour, raids in the night, and private quarrels that spilled over into the court. In particular, there was the strange case of the Earl of Bothwell (not Queen Mary's husband) who was accused of witchcraft and then attempted to abduct the King.

As often as he could, he returned to his own home at HalHill. On the birth of James and Anne's first son, Melville was detailed to entertain various ambassadors. The King of France failed to send an Ambassador, and Queen Elizabeth was so late in doing so, that the baptism was postponed, and Melville was ordered to keep the other ambassadors happy whilst James waited to hear from Elizabeth. He was then at the Queen's side as she graciously received the gifts from other countries.

In 1603, Elizabeth died, and James was proclaimed as James I of England. The majority of the court moved south, but Melville declined to go, finally retiring to Halhill, where he spent his time writings his memoirs, dying on 13th November 1617. The birth and death dates of his children are unknown, with the exception of his son Robert, who died in 1562.

## Aspects of Sir James Melville's Life

### Chapter 21: Links in a Chain

The word *'networking'* in the modern sense of expanding your influence by building relationships with a range of people who can support you, was not used in the sixteenth century. The concept, however, was at the heart of all political and family life.

No matter what stratum of society you were born into, the links of kinship and mutual obligation were cherished and reinforced, where possible, by marriage. It was expected that you would do a good turn for a family member, or someone recommended to you, and the recipient of your help, would, in turn, help you, or your family.

Similarly, if you quarrelled with someone, your *'affinity'* would be expected to quarrel too, leading to feuds lasting for generations.

In a small society, such as that of the Scottish Court, repeated intermarriages created a web of complex familial and patronage links. Without understanding these kinships, it can be very difficult to understand why certain factions coalesced or fought. Matters became even more complex in the mid-sixteenth century with the advent of the Reformation, which added a layer of religious agreement or dissent over old connections.

James Melville was no exception to the rule, and he was linked to many of the central players involved in the politics of the English and Scottish courts.

Starting with his family of birth, Melville had five brothers who survived to adulthood: John, Robert, David, William and Andrew, as well as three sisters. All six of the brothers had royal appointments. Robert and Andrew were both Masters of the Household to Queen Mary and James VI, William served the Prince of Orange, and Robert was also a long-serving ambassador at the English court. Andrew's first wife, Lady Jane Kennedy, was drowned in the storms that prevented the arrival of Anne of Denmark, and gave rise to the witchcraft trial of North Berwick. Lady Jane was probably the same Lady Jane Kennedy who attended Mary, Queen of Scots to her execution.

Both Robert and Andrew remained faithful to Queen Mary. Robert was besieged with other members of the Queen's Party in Edinburgh Castle, as Sir William Kirkcaldy of Grange held out against the Regents Moray, Lennox, Mar and Morton. It is likely that Kirkcaldy was, in fact the Melvilles' brother-in-law, married to their sister Janet.

It seems straightforward, therefore, to assume that the Melvilles all supported the Queen's Party, but there were complications. Another sister, Margaret, was married to Lord Elphinstone, and he was a supporter of the Earl of Morton. When Morton was banished, following the murder of David Rizzio, in which he played a prominent part, Margaret asked Melville to plead for him.

More difficult to define were the relationships that Melville had with members of the English court. During his youth in France, a cohort of young, Protestant, Englishmen was also there, having gone into voluntary exile when Mary I came to the throne. Henri II of France, although quite as Catholic as Mary I, could not resist the opportunity to undermine the Queen of England by harbouring her enemies.

Amongst these young men who became friends of Melville were Nicholas Throckmorton of Coughton, and Henry Killigrew of Arwenack. Both Melville and his brother Robert became very close to Killigrew, and it is possible that Melville was married to one of his sisters. Killigrew himself was married to Katherine Cooke, whose sister, Mildred, was the wife of Sir William Cecil, Lord Burghley. Melville therefore had close contact, if not a family connection, with Queen Mary's most implacable enemy. Killigrew was so close to Cecil and Elizabeth, that he was the only one entrusted with their plan to hand Mary back to her Lords with a view to her being tried (and almost certainly executed) in Scotland.

Nicholas Throckmorton, senior to Killigrew in France, also played a role in Scottish politics. A cousin of Queen Katherine Parr, he was a strong adherent of the Reformed faith, yet he favoured Mary, Queen of Scot' right to succeed Elizabeth. Perhaps changing his mind, when Mary was deposed, he recommended Elizabeth support the rebel lords, but was later implicated in the Duke of Norfolk's plan to marry Mary.

Thomas Randolph was another friend of Melville's from the time Melville spent on the continent – they probably met in Germany, when Melville was in the service of the Elector Palatine, and Randolph was an English envoy. Randolph was trusted by the Protestant party in Scotland and had good relations with the Queen's half-brother, the Earl of Moray, who, although relied on by the Queen initially was certainly plotting behind her back, involved in both the murder of Rizzio, and the planning behind the death of Darnley. Melville and Randolph quarrelled when it appeared that Randolph was threatening to burn Melville's mother's land, in retaliation for attacks on the Regent Morton.

Another layer of obfuscation about motives and connections is added when the relationships between the various Regents of Scotland are considered. James Hamilton, Duke of Chatelherault (formerly the Earl of Arran) was considered to be the Queen's heir before the birth of her son. He was hated by his distant cousin, Lennox, who considered he had a greater right to the throne. When Lennox' son, Darnley, married the Queen, the Lennox star appeared to be rising.

On Darnley's death, Mary married the Earl of Bothwell, who was formerly brother-in-law to George Gordon, Earl of Huntly. Huntly and Moray were at daggers drawn, even though Huntly's wife was the aunt of Moray's wife.

Moray was half-brother to Morton's wife, who was Chatelherault's sister-in-law. Moray was also nephew to John Erskine, Earl of Mar, who succeeded Lennox as Regent. Lennox' wife, Lady Margaret Douglas, hated Morton, her first cousin, because her father's earldom of Angus had been bequeathed to his branch of the family...

These entangled relationships are just the tip of the iceberg – but it is quite impossible to understand what was going on in the politics of England and Scotland without knowing about these convoluted links. There were as well, all the usual human factors of affection, dislike, distrust and greed to mystify matters further.

## Chapter 22: Melville's Inheritance

On 9th February, 1570 Henry Balnaves died. Balnaves was a '*Senator of Our Sovereign Lord's College of Justice*', otherwise known as a Lord of Session. A native of Fife, Balnaves was born around 1502 but does not seem to have been of a particularly illustrious background. In 1526 he was enrolled in St Salvator's College, at the University of St Andrew's, suggesting that he was planning at one point to join the priesthood, as most university students did. Balnaves, however, specialised in law. After a period in the Low Countries and Cologne, during which he was converted to Protestantism, he returned to Scotland.

Back in Fife, he either became acquainted with, or renewed a friendship with Sir John Melville of Raith. Balnaves was employed as a treasurer by Sir James Kirkcaldy of Grange, whose wife was Sir John Melville's daughter, Janet. By 1537, he was an Advocate in front of the

Court of Session, becoming a Lord of Session on 31st July 1538. On 8th August 1539 he and his wife, Christian Scheves, acquired lands at Halhill, East Colessie, in Fife from Sir Alexander Cumming of Inverlochy, with an entail to their lawful children.

It does not appear that Balnaves had any children, and when he made his will on 3rd January 1570, he named his adopted son, James Melville, as his heir and executor. The estate that Melville inherited included:

Lands at Halhill, with barns and barnyard

16 drawing oxen, worth £5 6s 4d each

4 cows, two with calves worth £4 per head

2 unknown animals, perhaps stirks, worth 40s each

23 ewes at 15s each

34 pigs at 10s each

70 bolls of oats at 13s 4d (a boll was a Scots measure equal to 5 bushels 3 pecks in English measure or about 600kg in metric)

13 bolls of wheat at 30s each (c. 108kg)

10 bolls of peas at 20s (c. 75 kg)

27 bolls of beer at 26s 4d each (possibly around 35 barrels in modern measurements of 36 gallons to the barrel)

Household goods and utensils to the value of £26 13s 8d.

Outstanding debts owed to the estate, for rent and crops £147 8s.

The whole estate was worth £421 6s 8d Scots (about £105 English) from which Melville was to pay various bequests, including £10 to the poor of Edinburgh.

Balnaves' best damask gown, lined with velvet, was left to Melville's wife, Christian Boswell, who was, perhaps, a relative of Mrs Balnaves.

We can infer this because Mrs Balnaves left £12 to a lady named Helen Boswell.  The remainder of Balnaves' silk clothes were left to Melville, and various other small bequests of money and clothes to family and friends.

To give an idea of the purchasing power of the money in 2015, a farm and buildings in Fife today would cost in the region of £600,000 – 700,000.

On the death of Melville in 1617, the lands passed to his eldest son, another James, but his direct descendants had died out by the early 18th century.

### Chapter 23: Following the Footsteps of James Melville

Melville spent much of his youth in France, before journeying to the courts of European rulers, on behalf of the various men and women he served.  Once back in Scotland, he travelled around Lowland Scotland with the Scottish Court as well as making several journeys south to the court of Elizabeth I.

The numbers in the article below correspond to those on the map which follows.

*

Melville was born in Raith (1), in Fife. Raith today is a suburb of Kirkcaldy, a pretty sea-side town with an unusually long sea-front.  Fife was one of the first areas of Scotland to follow the Reformed faith, and the legacy has lasted through the centuries.  Former British Prime Minister, Gordon Brown, son of the Presbyterian Minister of Kirkcaldy, sat for the Parliamentary seat from 1983 – 2015.

Melville's father, Sir John, was Captain of Dunbar Castle, but it is unlikely Melville went there during early childhood, although he knew it later.  Together with his six brothers and three sisters, he probably remained at home.

In 1548, Sir John was executed for treason and his lands forfeit.  It is not apparent exactly what provision was made for his children, but James and his older brother, Robert, were soon found court appointments.  Marie of Guise, mother of the young Mary, Queen of Scots and later Regent, sent Robert to France with the Queen in 1548, and the following year, James, too, was sent there.

He travelled in the train of the Bishop of Vallance, and their first port of call was Ireland, which they reached after considerable time at sea, tossed by storms.  They spent three weeks there, then returned to Dumbarton Castle (2).  Dumbarton, one of the strongest forts in Scotland, is on the mouth of the River Clyde, and the usual sailing point for France by the western route.  Dumbarton today is largely an 18th and 19th century structure, but its origins are a thousand years older, it having been the capital of the old Celtic kingdom of Strathclyde.

Following a brief visit to Stirling Castle (3) (well worth a visit to see the royal apartments) to report to Queen Marie on affairs in Ireland, the party set sail again, landing in France some three weeks later, battered again by storms.

Whilst in France, Melville fought at the Battle of St Quentin, now in the department of Aisne in Picardy, not far from the Belgian border.  He was present at the negotiation of the peace treaty agreed after the battle at Le Cateau-Cambresis, near Bordeaux.

In the next couple of years Melville made a number of journeys around Europe.  His first trip was a return home in 1559.  It appears that, whenever possible, Melville travelled by land, and so on this occasion, he travelled via England.  Probably the initial awful journey to France put him off sailing.  He attended Queen Marie at Falkland Palace (4) in his native Fife.  Falkland today is an extremely well preserved palace, open to the public and with many traces of the occupation of Marie of Guise, and James V.

Travelling back to France, Melville would have travelled down what is now the A1 – The Great North Road from London to Edinburgh. He stopped en route in Newcastle (5), whose Norman Castle overshadowed the small town at its foot. The Castle is open to the public, and gives a good idea of what life in the Borders was like, when Scotland and England were frequently at war.

Back on the continent, Melville travelled to the court of the Frederick III, Elector Palatine, in Heidelburg, and then on various embassies for Frederick, including to the court of Maximillian, King of the Romans, and soon to be Emperor, at Innsbruck. He also visited Venice and Rome, but left no information about his opinion of those cities.

He left the service of the Elector, to join that of Mary, Queen of Scots, who had returned to Scotland in 1561. On Mary's behalf, he undertook a couple of embassies to the court of Elizabeth I, attending Elizabeth at Hampton Court (6) on the first occasion. Hampton Court is open to the public and is one of the greatest palaces in England – don't miss an opportunity to see it!

On a subsequent visit he went to Westminster Palace (9). The only fragment of the original Westminster Palace to remain is Westminster Hall, whose great hammer-beam roof dates from the reign of Richard II. The palace Melville would have known burnt down in the Great Fire of 1834. The current Houses of Parliament stand more-or-less where the Palace was. Westminster Hall may be visited as part of a booked tour.

Mary's court moved around Scotland, and Melville attended her at St Johnstone, near Perth (7), where the castle had been in royal hands since the time of Robert the Bruce. Although there are other castles nearby, nothing remains of Perth Castle.

The Queen's favourite palace in Edinburgh was Holyroodhouse, largely built by her grandfather, James IV, and father, James V. It was the burial location of James V, and Mary's two elder brothers, who had died as infants. It was here that she married Lord Darnley on 29th July, 1565, a match approved of by Melville.

Holyroodhouse, the current Queen's official residence in Scotland, is delightfully situated in Edinburgh, surrounded by gardens, and with views to Arthur's Seat, the crag overlooking the city. It was here that the shocking murder of David Rizzio, Mary's secretary took place, in front of the pregnant Queen.

Mary retreated to Dunbar in East Lothian, where Melville's father had been Captain of the Castle, but then emerged and spent a short period at Haddington (11), where she instructed Melville to write letters summoning her estranged half-brother, Moray, home.

Mary, fearful for her own safety and that of her unborn child, chose the great fortress of Edinburgh Castle (9) to give birth to Prince James in 1566. Melville waited outside her apartments to hear of her delivery, before setting off for London to inform Elizabeth I. He reached Berwick (12) the same day. Berwick-upon-Tweed, now a small, pretty town, on the north side of the Tweed is one of the most fought over locations in British history. By the sixteenth century, it had settled into English hands, and was the location where many conferences and meetings took place between diplomats of both sides. Nevertheless, the border was not secure and a new encircling wall was built by the English, which may be seen today.

Four days after setting out with his good news, Melville arrived in London, and travelled down the river to make his announcement to Elizabeth at Greenwich (13). The site of the palace at Greenwich, called Placentia, is now covered by what were once the Royal Naval College buildings and is now the University of Greenwich.

Melville's last known trip out of Scotland was in 1568. Mary had been defeated at the Battle of Langside, and had escaped (or so she thought) into England. Alas, she was now trapped. Elizabeth, wishing neither to free her, nor condemn her, set up a Commission to investigate the murder of Darnley. Melville was present at its deliberations in both York and Hampton Court.

Following this last journey, although Melville travelled extensively between the royal palaces and castles in Scotland, he refused all commissions to travel further than Berwick. He spent as much time as he could at his home of Halhill, near Collessie, in Fife, where he was buried in 1617 in a Church where his vault, built by him in 1609, may still be seen, following extensive restoration. The inscription on the tomb reads (with a couple of interpolations where the text is unclear)

*'Ye loadin pilgrims passing langs this way*
*Pans [think] on your fall your offences past*
*How your frail flesh first formit of the clay*
*In dust mon [must] be desovit at the last*
*Repent amen on Christ the burden cast*
*Of your sad sinnes who can your sauls [souls] refresh*
*Syne [since] rais from grave to gloir your grislie flesh*
*Defyle not Christs kirk with your carrion*
*A solemn seat for Gods service prepared*
*For prayer preaching and communion*
*Your burial should be in the kirkyard*
*On your uprising set your great regard*
*When saul and body ioynes [joins] with joy to ring*
*In heave for ay [ever] with Christ over head and king.'*

The question of whether burial should take place in the Church (Catholic practice) or the Churchyard (Protestant practice) was a vexed one at the time, and Melville is confirming his Protestant views.

Key to Map

1. Raith, Fife, Scotland
2. Dumbarton Castle, Clyde & Ayrshire, Scotland
3. Stirling Castle, Stirling, Scotland
4. Falkland Palace, Fife, Scotland
5. Newcastle, Tyne & Wear, England
6. Hampton Court, nr Kingston, England
7. St Johnston, nr Perth, Perthshire, Scotland
8. Edinburgh Castle, Edinburgh, Scotland
9. Westminster Palace, London, England
10. Holyrood Palace, Edinburgh, Scotland
11. Haddington, East Lothian, Scotland
12. Berwick-upon-Tweed, Northumberland, England
13. Greenwich, London, England
14. York, North Yorkshire, England
15. Halhill, Collessie, Fife, Scotland

No trace

In Current Use

Later Replaced

## Chapter 24: Book Review

There are no biographies about James Melville himself, so we have chosen a third account of the reign of Mary, Queen of Scots to compare with the other two, previously reviewed ('*My Heart is My Own*' by John Guy on page 253 and '*Crown of Thistles*' by Linda Porter on page 384). In '*The Challenge to the Crown*', Robert Stedall brings a different perspective to events.

*The Challenge to the Crown: The Struggle for Influence in the Reign of Mary, Queen of Scots 1542 – 1567*

Author: Robert Stedall

Publisher: The Book Guild Ltd

**In a nutshell** A detailed analysis of the plots, and counterplots that characterised the reign of Mary, Queen of Scots, with credible insight into the complex motivations of those involved.

Mr Stedall did not begin his career as a professional historian, but that does not handicap his ability to pick his way through the complex politics at the court of Mary, Queen of Scots. He begins the narrative with a description of the situation in Scotland in the early 1540s – the King dead, the struggle for the Regency, and the looming threat of England. He then carries us into France with the little Queen, sent there for safety, aged 5. Stedall covers Mary's childhood and education in some detail. There is useful information about the politics of France, peppered with some of the more scandalous details of the French courts' love affairs, and background about Catherine de Medici.

He examines the political implications of the marriage of Mary to the Dauphin of Scotland, and that the ceding of the Crown Matrimonial to François meant that Mary's natural heir, the Duke of Chatelherault, and his son the Earl of Arran were given a reason to join the Lords of the Congregation in their opposition to the Regency of Mary's mother. As Mary grew to adulthood in France, Scotland's elite, with the exception of her mother, the Queen-Regent, were turning away from the Auld Alliance with Catholic France, and seeking to join in common cause with Protestant England.

Stedwall gives an excellent summary of the position in Scotland and the alignment of the various factions on Mary's return as a widow from France. He makes it clear that combination in factions was not just a religious matter. The Catholic Huntly and the Protestant Bothwell were both opposed to the Protestant Moray, who was pro an alliance with England. Stedall, unlike many other writers, believes that Moray always entertained ambitions to snatch his half-sister's throne, but was willing to content himself with being her chief advisor, until the advent of her second husband, Lord Darnley.

In describing her reign, Stedall concludes that Mary, whilst clever and astute in many ways, and adept at gathering personal support 'showed political naivety and a misjudgement of people'. He also convincingly demonstrates that her marriage to Darnley was a headstrong act, undertaken almost entirely without support from any of her nobles and saddled her with a fatal liability.

Stedall takes a different approach to the murder of Rizzio, from that espoused by John Guy in 'My Heart is My Own'. (see page 253). It is Stedall's contention that Darnley intended Mary and their unborn child to die after the shock of witnessing the murder, with the goal of claiming the Crown himself, through his own Stewart blood (although the Duke of Chatelherault was widely accepted as the next heir).

The narrative of Darnley's death is complex, as the subject itself is complex. Stedall's view is that Mary was innocent of the murder, and the whole plot was masterminded by Moray from start to finish, with Bothwell being manipulated into thinking it his own idea, and actually arranging it. Mary is shown as walking into the trap of appearing to be complicit in the murder of Darnley and her apparent abduction, by being too shamed by having slept with Bothwell (whether willingly or not) to refuse to marry him. Stedall concludes, however, that Mary's own failure to listen to sensible advice, and her stupidity in marrying Bothwell, despite it being evident that he had been involved in Darnley's murder, were the ultimate causes of her downfall.

This first volume in a two-volume work ends with Mary's deposition and Moray's acceptance as Regent.

Stendall's style is readable, and I received the impression that he knew the details of his subject well. Where the writer's inexperience perhaps shows is in a few places where the narrative becomes confused. Occasionally, lots of pronouns rather than names mean it is unclear exactly who was doing what to whom – the tendency of all the participants in the politics of the 1550s and 1560s to change sides and betray each other making it difficult to infer the identities from the context.

Annoyingly, the Kindle version of the book has jumbled footnotes that merge into the text.

## Bibliography

*Accounts of the Treasurer of Scotland: v. 5-8:*. Edinburgh: H.M. General Register House, 1877

*Calendar of Border Papers: Volume 1, 1560-95* <http://www.british-history.ac.uk/cal-border-papers/vol1/> [accessed 12 November 2015]

*Calendar of State Papers: Scotland* <http://www.british-history.ac.uk/cal-state-papers/scotland> [accessed 10 November 2015]

*Calendar of State Papers: Domestic Series: Edward VI, 1547-1553.* United Kingdom: Stationery Office Books.

*Calendar of State Papers: Domestic: Mary I 1553-1558.* London: Public Record Office.

*Calendar of State Papers Simancas*, British History Online (HMSO, 1892) Hume, Martin A S, ed.,

*Calendar of State Papers: Venice* <http://www.british-history.ac.uk/cal-state-papers/venice/vol2/vii-lxi> [accessed 7 October 2015]

*Cecil      Papers*,      http://www.british-history.ac.uk/cal-cecil-papers (Accessed: 7 September 2015)

Melville, James Sir and Donaldson, Gordon (ed), *The Memoirs of Sir James Melville of Halhill, Containing an Impartial Account of the Most Remarkable Affairs of State during the Sixteenth Century Not Mentioned by Other Historians, More Particularly Relating to the Kingdoms of England and Scotland under the reigns of Queen Elizabeth, Mary Queen of Scots and King James* (London: Folio Society, 1969)

*Records of the Parliaments of Scotland* <http://www.rps.ac.uk/> [accessed 17 September 2015]

http://www.scottishgraveyards.org.uk/downloads/16Collessie.pdf> [accessed 9 November 2015]

De Lisle, Leanda, *Tudor: The Family Story* (United Kingdom: Chatto & Windus, 2013)

Drummond, William, ed., *The History of Scotland from the Year 1423 until the Year 1542, Containing the Lives and Reigns of James I, II, III, IV and V* (London: H Hills for R Tomlins and himself, 1655)

Foxe, John, *The Acts and Monuments of John Foxe: A New and Complete Edition: With a Preliminary Dissertation by the Rev. George Townsend* (London: R.R. Seeley and W. Burnside, 1837)

Fraser, Antonia, *Mary Queen of Scots* (London: HarperCollins Publishers, 1970)

Guy, J. (2004) *My Heart is My Own: the Life of Mary Queen of Scots.* London: Harper Perennial.

Holinshed, Raphael, *Holinshed's Chronicles of England, Scotland & Ireland* (United Kingdom: AMS Press, 1997)

Keith, Robert: *History of the Affairs of Church and State in Scotland from the Beginning of the Reformation to the Year 1568* (Edinburgh: Spottiswoode, 1844)

Knox, John, *The Works of John Knox* Vols 1 - 6, ed. by David Laing (United Kingdom: James Thin, 1895)

Lang, Andrew, *The History of Scotland from the Roman Occupation: Vol III C. 79 - 1545*, 3rd edn (New York: Dodd, Mead & Co., 1903)

Lemon, Robert, ed., *Calendar of State Papers: Domestic Series: Edward, Mary and Elizabeth,* British History Online (London: HMSO, 1856)

Leslie, John, The History of Scotland: From the Death of King James I, in the Year 1436 to 1561 (United States: Kessinger Publishing, 2007)

Lindsay of Pitscottie, Robert, *Pitscottie's Chronicles of Scotland*, ed. by Ae. J. G Mackay (Edinburgh: Blackwood for the Society, 1911)

MacDonald, Stuart, *The Witches of Fife: Witch-Hunting in a Scottish Shire 1560 - 1710*, Kindle (Edinburgh: John Donald Publishers, 2002)

Marshall, R. K. (2003) *Scottish Queens 1034 - 1714*. United Kingdom: Tuckwell Press.

Marshall, Rosalind Kay, *Queen Mary's Women: Female Relatives, Servants, Friends and Enemies of Mary, Queen of Scots* (Edinburgh: John Donald Publishers, 2006)

Oliver, Neil: *A History of Scotland* (Phoenix PR, 2011)

Porter, Linda, *Crown of Thistles: The Fatal Inheritance of Mary Queen of Scots* (United Kingdom: Macmillan, 2013)

Ritchie, P. E. (2002) *Mary of Guise in Scotland, 1548-1560: A Political Study*. United Kingdom: Tuckwell Press.

Sadler, Sir Ralph, *The State Papers and Letters of Sir Ralph Sadler in 3 Volumes*, ed. by Arthur Clifford (Edinburgh: Archibald Constable & Co., 1809)

Stedall, Robert, *The Challenge to the Crown: The Struggle for Influence in the Reign of Mary, Queen of Scots 1542 - 1567*, 1st edn (Sussex, England: Book Guild Publishing, 2012)

Strickland, Agnes: *Lives Of The Queens Of Scotland And English Princesses: Connected With The Regal Succession Of Great Britain* (Harper & Brothers, 1859), i & ii

Thomson, John Maitland, ed., *The Register of the Great Seal of Scotland* (Edinburgh: HM General Register House, 1894)

www.ingramcontent.com/pod-product-compliance
Lightning Source LLC
Chambersburg PA
CBHW021218020426
42331CB00003B/368